Robert H. Collyer

Mysteries of the Vital Element in Connexion with Dreams, Somnambulism, Trance, Vital Photography, Faith and Will, Anaesthesia, Nervous Congestion and Creative Function

Modern Spiritualism Explained

Robert H. Collyer

Mysteries of the Vital Element in Connexion with Dreams, Somnambulism, Trance, Vital Photography, Faith and Will, Anaesthesia, Nervous Congestion and Creative Function
Modern Spiritualism Explained

ISBN/EAN: 9783337428303

Printed in Europe, USA, Canada, Australia, Japan

Cover: Foto ©Lupo / pixelio.de

More available books at **www.hansebooks.com**

MYSTERIES

OF

THE VITAL ELEMENT

IN CONNEXION WITH

DREAMS, SOMNAMBULISM, TRANCE,
VITAL PHOTOGRAPHY, FAITH AND WILL, ANÆSTHESIA,
NERVOUS CONGESTION AND CREATIVE FUNCTION.

MODERN SPIRITUALISM EXPLAINED.

BY

ROBERT H. COLLYER, M.D.

REGISTERED BY THE COUNCIL OF MEDICAL EDUCATION.

Original Discoverer of Anæsthesia by the Inhalation of Narcotic and Stimulating Vapours, Discoverer of Electro-biology, Author of *The Physiology of the Brain and Nervous System*; Graduate of the Berkshire Medical College, Massachusetts; Member of the Massachusetts Medical Society; formerly Student of the London and Paris Schools of Medicine; late Principal Physician to the Cholera Hospital, Mexico.

"Divinum est opus sedare dolorum."—HIPPOCRATES.

"Dr. Collyer, to our minds, is the true modern pioneer, after all—the man who ran first."
LANCET, *June 11th*, 1870.

SECOND EDITION.

HENRY RENSHAW,
356, STRAND, LONDON.

1871.

CONTENTS.

CHAPTER I.
ANÆSTHESIA 1

CHAPTER II.
CONTENDING CLAIMS OF HORACE WELLS, WM. T. G. MORTON, AND DR. CHARLES T. JACKSON. 16

CHAPTER III.
CONTENDING CLAIMS OF WM. T. G. MORTON AND DR. C. T. JACKSON . 23

CHAPTER IV.
ANÆSTHESIA IN EUROPE 29

CHAPTER V.
ANIMAL MAGNETISM, MESMERISM, OR NERVOUS CONGESTION, AND OTHER ALLIED TOPICS 48

CHAPTER VI.
EGYPTIAN MYSTERIES 57

CHAPTER VII.
SOMNAMBULISM 60

CHAPTER VIII.
DREAMS AND ABNORMAL BRAIN AND VITAL FUNCTION 72

CONTENTS.

CHAPTER IX.
VITAL PHOTOGRAPHY 78

CHAPTER X.
CREATIVE FUNCTION 86

CHAPTER XI.
FAITH AND WILL 92

CHAPTER XII.
MODERN SPIRITUALISM 102

APPENDIX.

CHRONOLOGICAL HISTORY OF ANÆSTHESIA 111
REPORT OF BOSTON COMMITTEE 112
WELLS'S LETTER TO GALIGNANI 121
DR. COLLYER'S LETTER TO LONDON CRITIC 123
OFFICIAL MEXICAN DOCUMENT 126
LETTER FROM DR. HENRY BENNET 127
LETTER TO DR. B. W. RICHARDSON 128
LETTER TO SIR JAMES Y. SIMPSON 129
CERTIFICATE OF COPYRIGHT IN 1843 135
REVIEW OF LANCET'S ARTICLE OF JUNE 11TH, 1870 135
CHLOROFORM AND METHYLENE 143

PREFATORY REMARKS.

IN presenting to the medical profession a second edition of "The History of Anæsthetic Discovery," it is with the conviction that it will be received with the same indulgent and liberal spirit which characterized the reception of the first imperfect edition, published in Bruges 1868.

That the development of modern Anæsthesia should have been closely associated with that condition of insensibility induced by the mesmeric process or "nervous congestive state of brain," cannot excite astonishment when it is remembered that the first authentically recorded anæsthetic surgical operation was performed as early as April, 1829, by the eminent French surgeon, Jules Cloquet, who removed the cancerous breast of a lady who had been rendered unconscious, in view of the operation being painless. It was the knowledge of this fact which induced me to repeat in 1841, the nervous congestive or mesmeric comatose state in a child only twenty-two months, so that a fungus, involving the globe of the eye, might be extirpated painlessly. The entire success of this wonderful operation at the time, on a child of such tender age, put the question of producing an anæsthetic state beyond the possibility of a doubt, and encouraged further research. Prior to this, in December, 1839, I had reduced a dislocation of the femur, in a negro who had been rendered anæsthetic by the INHALATION of the vapours from alcohol. In 1835, I, when a student at the London University College, was rendered unconscious by the inhalation of ether, in the chemical lecture room of Dr. Turner.

It was the combination of these facts which eventually led to the discovery of anæsthesia, by the inhalation of narcotic and stimulating vapours. Important documentary evidence confirmatory of the first surgical operation, in December, 1839, and also of the first experiments in producing unconsciousness by "*the inhalation of narcotic and stimu-*

PREFATORY REMARKS.

lating vapours," were lost in Mexico in July, 1849, when the author was attacked by banditti in the Sierra Madre Mountains, and in San Francisco, at the great fire of May, 1851. These documents form the basis of the letter published in the *Critic*, April 10th, 1847 (No. 119), where these words are used:—"*Had I not been prevented in consequence of illness, I would long since have visited London with my publications.*"

The official certificates from the Mexican authorities, attesting to the loss of the documents referred to, are now in my possession, the copy of which will be found in the Appendix.

Sufficient evidence has, however, been preserved to put all contending claims out of court, as the existing documents of 1842 and 1843 antedate all others by several years.

If the reader deems the contents too personal, too much of self, or too severe, he must remember that for nearly a quarter of a century I have been *defrauded* of my just rights as the original discoverer; every species of misrepresentation and special pleading has been resorted to to deceive and mislead the public. These proceedings will be thoroughly exposed; and if the parties implicated are severely dealt with, I hope that in so doing I shall never deviate from the strictest path of truth.

When the rival claims of Horace Wells, W. T. G. Morton, and Dr. Charles T. Jackson were presented to the Committee of the House of Representatives, Washington, in 1851 and 1852, I was in California. I, however, sent sufficient proof to some leading members of Congress, as to my priority, which defeated the claims of the contending parties.

The Hon. Truman Smith, in his "Modern Anæsthesia," says, "Shall imposture be permitted to usurp the place of merit? Shall ignorance and presumption over-top the emanations of true genius, and all promptings of a generous self-sacrificing spirit? Shall artifice, chicanery, and mendacity stand before sincerity, rectitude, truth, and honour?"

When these pages have been carefully read and the dates noted, the reader will be in a position to answer these questions with an unbiassed mind.

Dr. Richardson having published a lecture on the "Nervous Atmosphere" in the *Medical Times* of May 6th, 1871, I am particularly anxious, as a stranger, to impress on the public mind that my ideas relative to the nervous fluid have not been copied, or in any way prejudiced by the publication of Dr. Richardson. In fine, we both treat the matter *originally*.

The manuscript forming this volume was in the possession of the

PREFATORY REMARKS.

publisher, Mr. Renshaw, in February, 1871. In the original, the whole theory of the *nervous atmosphere* is propounded.

It is at all times a most onerous and distasteful task to be necessitated to vindicate one's self in relation to being a discoverer, after a lapse of years has been allowed to pass, during which time the palm has been justly or unjustly accorded to others. It is most difficult to turn the channel of thought when once established in the public mind. This conviction has caused personal details to be discussed with which I am familiar, in order to substantiate the facts which prove incontrovertibly who was the original discoverer of the anæsthetic process. Circumstances of an exceptional and peculiar character have been the cause of the *apparent* neglect, in allowing so important a discovery to be awarded to others. I have, however, persistently from 1847 to the present date, taken every opportunity through the medium of the press in the United States and Great Britain, of publicly maintaining my claim to priority.

In fine, no great discovery has been made without its having to contend against all the prejudices and bigotry of the age. When once, however, recognised, there are not wanting men who would fain take the merit to themselves, or who, on the principle or law of nature having been established, are not slow to render themselves distinguished at the expense of the original discoverer.

It should not be forgotten that both Dr. Jackson and Mr. Morton have always *denied* the anæsthetic properties of nitrous oxide even as late as 1862. It is not asking too much of the profession now, in 1871, to consider if I had not known of its properties, as published in the *Critic*, in April, 1847, to produce anæsthesia, how was it possible for me to have arrived at so *definite* a conclusion, which is stated without any reserve, had I not made the experiments at a prior date? *Vide* also *London Critic*, January 6th, 1847.

In conclusion, I ask of the profession and the public the strictest justice and impartiality, as to awarding me the honour of having been the original discoverer that the inhalation of narcotic and stimulating vapours produced an anæsthetic state so that surgical operations could be painlessly performed.

If any one can produce a publication anterior to that made by me in 1843, then all controversy must cease, but until then I claim the undivided right of being recognised as *the discoverer*.

It was not originally intended that this publication should have comprised other matter than that of the Anæsthetic Discovery. It has, however, been found, as the investigation necessarily involved

PREFATORY REMARKS.

various physiological conditions of brain function, such as *Nervous Congestion, Sleep, Sleeplessness, Dreams, Somnambulism, Hybernation, Mental Hallucination, Vital Photography, Creative Function*, and many other topics of equal interest, that the extension of the work including these would be acceptable, more particularly as the various abnormal phenomena of brain function have been treated in a popular manner, purposely avoiding all technical phraseology, so that the unprofessional reader may more clearly comprehend the ideas advanced.

ROBERT H. COLLYER, M.D.

LONDON,
199, BROMPTON ROAD, S.W.
Near South Kensington Museum.
June 1st, 1871.

NOTICE.

DR. COLLYER is engaged in the prosecution of a series of experiments on the *vital element*, with a view to the publication of—

MYSTERIA REVELATA:

OR,

THE FUNCTIONS OF THE NERVOUS SYSTEM ARTIFICIALLY INDUCED.

Whenever the phenomena incidental to these investigations—with *the Vital Battery*—present so definite and undeniable a character as to be witnessed without the possibility of a doubt being raised as to their genuineness, the Subscribers to the work will be communicated with. A Subscription List is open at Mr. Renshaw's, 356, Strand, and at 199, Brompton Road, near South Kensington Museum.

MYSTERIES OF THE VITAL ELEMENT,

ETC.

CHAPTER I.

ANÆSTHESIA.

ANÆSTHESIA, is the faculty of rendering the nervous system insensible to outward impressions; during the state thus induced, surgical operations and the most difficult parturitions are devoid of physical suffering. It is the realization of a mythical and poetical dream, which has occupied the mind of man from the earliest ages of his civilization. The abolition of *pain*, the annihilation of human suffering during the most distressing moments of existence, is indeed a boon, a blessing, which, to trace through all the degrees of its development, must claim our gratitude, as it must interest our curiosity.

Has not the terror of agonized pain, in its most excruciating forms, been painted with artistic power on the imagination of the ignorant, as the representative condition, associated with a state of those *who are damned*—the poor wretches who are condemned to purgatory, or, worse, to an everlasting state of physical torture? Science has indeed achieved a lasting triumph in the annihilation of pain.

Man's ignorance of the laws which govern his well-being has always made him the victim of disease. He too, is always liable to accidents, or, from a still more inexplicable perversity or obtuseness, he is led to mortal combat against his fellow-men. All kinds of mutilations and injuries follow. The Anæsthetic discovery is made available to render him *unconscious*, so that the surgeon may repair to the best advantage the diseased or mutilated parts.

It is to the medical profession, that the world is indebted for the accomplishment of the inestimable blessing of inducing insensibility " by the inhalation of narcotic and stimulating vapours."

The vestiges of early history show, that the art of producing *a*

ANÆSTHESIA.

comatose state was connected with the mysterious ceremonies and customs of the priest and the magician.

The Egyptians, in their ceremonies of initiation into the mysteries, used a soporific cake, " composed of honey and medicated grains," (*medicatis frugibus*). In the mysteries of Trophonius (who was said to have been nursed by Ceres, that is, to have derived his rites from the Eleusinian), the initiated carried the same sort of medicated cake to appease the serpents (Pythons) they met in their passage, so as to cast them into *a slumber*. Tertullian, who attributes all the mysteries to the devil, and makes him the author of what passes there, mentions the offering of these cakes, "celebrat et panis oblationem." This was, no doubt, made of poppy seeds with honey, the same as the medicatis frugibus. The priestess of Venus is made to prepare the same treat for the dragon who guarded the Hesperian fruit. The poppy juice was always given to those, who were to undergo the ceremony of initiation into the mysteries. Plutarch speaks of a shrub called Leucophyllus, used in the celebration of the mysteries of Hecate, which threw men into a kind of frenzy, and made them confess their innermost thoughts. Medicine, priestcraft, and magic were practised only by those who had entered the temple.

The Greeks, who borrowed their ceremonies and practices from the Egyptians, used the Atropa Mandragora to allay pain. Some persons, according to Dioscorides, and his commentator Matthiolus, "boil the "root of mandrake in wine down to a third part, and preserve the "decoction, of which they administer a cyathus (about a fluid ounce and "a half), to produce sleep, and to allay severe pains of any part; and "also before operations with the knife, or the application of the actual "cautery, that the operation should not be felt."

Dodineus also affirms that if the wine of mandrake be administered before the application of the cautery, no pain is experienced.

A celebrated Chinese physician, Moatho, about the third century, gave to his patients a preparation of Cannabis Indica. In a short time they became insensible, during which state he made incisions, amputations, or removed the cause of disease.

Pliny mentions that Roman surgeons employed a marble powder from Cairo called Memphetis. This powder, he says, when mixed with vinegar, causes such numbness to the parts where it is applied, that it can be cut or cauterized without the patient feeling the least pain (*obstupescit ita corpus nec sentit cruciatum*).

Dioscorides recalls the same fact, and says, this stone of Memphis,

ANÆSTHESIA.

so used, is of the size of a talent, greasy to the feel, and of different colours; but this stone, once so celebrated, was soon forgotten.

It is evident, that a powder of marble, when mixed with acetic acid, would have the effect of deadening a part to which it is applied. The evolution of carbonic acid in a nascent state is a powerful local anæsthetic.

Haschisch—Indian hemp—has been used from the time of the early Egyptians; also by the Greeks and Scythians; according to Herodotus, these people were in the habit of inhaling the fumes until it produced a species of intoxication. In the thirteenth century, Theodorus a monk, afterwards a surgeon of great reputation, had learnt from Hugues de Lucques, by whom he had been instructed, the composition of a preparation, having for its object the mitigation of pain during surgical operations, (*confectio soporis a chirurgia facienda secundum hominis Hugonem*); this compound threw the patient into a state of insensibility. Its composition was opium, suc Morellæ, hyoscyamus, mandragora, and lactuca. The surgeon saturated a sponge with this liquid and allowed it to dry in the sun, and when it was required to be used it was moistened with hot water, and placed under the nose until the desired sleep was induced. After the operation, another sponge immersed in vinegar was applied to the nostrils, so as to revive the patient from the slumber induced.

During the fourteenth, fifteenth, and sixteenth centuries, various methods were resorted to, to render the patient insensible, but the results seem to have fallen into disuse. Some used compression on the course of the nerves.

It was not, however, until the 11th of April, 1799, that the illustrious chemist and philosopher, Sir Humphry Davy, the discoverer of protoxide of nitrogen, inhaled this gas, in order to assuage the pain incidental to cutting a tooth. He used these prophetic words:—"As " nitrous oxide, amongst its other properties, has that of destroying " physical pain, it may probably be employed with advantage during " surgical operations in which there is no great effusion of " blood."

The experiments of Sir Humphry Davy were soon repeated by the Medical Society of Toulouse, who found the effects to vary according to the individuals who inhaled the gas. The surgeon did not avail himself of its aid, but the experiments were continued in all the chemical schools and those of medicine, as exhibiting the exhilarating effects of the gas on the brain when inhaled. In the course of time, sulphuric ether was used as a substitute to produce similar agreeable sensations when inhaled. The *production* of a state of nervous congestion or unconsciousness was never dreamt of.

On the 12th April, 1829, Dr. Jules Cloquet, of Paris, performed a capital surgical operation on a lady, who was rendered anæsthetic by the nervous force or fluid. These are the facts:—

Dr. Chapelain magnetized a lady, who, having a cancer of the breast, an operation was considered indispensable to save her life. She was thrown into a deep sleep.* She then undressed herself and took a seat in an arm-chair, sustaining the operation of the entire extirpation of the breast, which lasted twelve minutes, without the least manifestation of pain. On being awakened some time afterwards, she had not the least recollection of what had taken place. The operator, Dr. Jules Cloquet, is the Professor of Anatomy in the Paris School of Medicine, and member of the Institute of France.

This, certainly, ought to have aroused the profession to the subject of Anæsthesia. Yet no one seemed to have repeated this successful operation commenced under such auspices.

After thirteen years, that is, in December, 1841, the second recorded surgical operation was performed on a child twenty-two months old, who had a fungus involving the left eye. The infant in twenty minutes was reduced to a perfectly comatose state. Dr. Rich, of Bangor, assisted by Drs. Dean and Fogg, operated, removing the entire globe and the fungus of large size in thirty-five minutes. The child did not manifest the least indication of physical suffering.

The following is from *The Bostonian*, April 23rd, 1842 :—

"Whilst Dr. Collyer was at Bangor, Dr. Dean, a physician of that "place, requested Dr. Collyer to visit a child in a town sixteen miles "distant. He consented, and they went, in company with Dr. Rich, an "eminent surgeon at Bangor. When they arrived at the house, the "mother had the child in her arms; its condition was dreadful, there "was a scrofulous tumour or ulcer the size of a large hen's egg covering "one of its eyes, and a surgical operation was necessary. Dr. Collyer "took the child and mesmerized it, so as to deprive it of all sensibility. "Dr. Rich then performed the operation of cutting out the entire eye, "which lasted thirty-five minutes, during which time the child did not "exhibit any feeling of pain." Numerous other cases were mentioned.

Two years prior to this, a surgical operation was performed, perhaps

---

* And the Lord God caused a deep sleep to fall on Adam, and he slept, and he took one of his ribs and closed up the flesh instead thereof.—*Genesis*, chapter ii. verse 21.

ANÆSTHESIA. 5

the first under a condition of unconsciousness, by the "*inhalation of narcotic and stimulating vapours.*"

This occurred on a plantation on the banks of the Mississippi, opposite Carrolton, some six miles above New Orleans. My dear father, in connexion with M. Laurent Millaudon, worked a large distillery on shares, which, during the season could produce 3000 gallons of rum daily. My father had on many occasions observed that the negroes attached to the distillery were much excited and seemed half-intoxicated, and as the distillery was closed on these occasions, he was much puzzled as to how they obtained the liquor. One Sunday afternoon, whilst lying on his sofa, smoking a cigar, in December, 1839, he heard a sudden burst of laughter coming from the interior of the distillery. Being astonished at so unusual an occurrence, having the key in his possession, he unlocked the door, when a scene met his view more easily imagined than described. Some eight negroes were in the act of attempting to raise one of their comrades, "Bob," who lay helpless and insensible on the floor. On instituting an enquiry, the mystery was soon unravelled; it seemed that the negroes had effected an entry into the distillery underneath the brick foundation, which led into a dilapidated "beer reservoir." When once inside, nothing was more easy than raising the trap-door common to each reservoir in the floor of the distillery.

The exterior entrance was kept carefully concealed with brushwood and shrubbery which grows so rapidly and luxuriantly in that climate. When a favourable opportunity presented itself, the negroes were in the habit of treating themselves to a *private inhalation*, which was accomplished by mounting the sides of the large vats containing the rectified spirits: they partially removed the cover, so as to put their heads under the canvas which surrounded the top of the vat. There they would inhale the rum atmosphere, experiencing the exhilarating effects of partial intoxication, which were similar to the breathing of nitrous oxide gas. On this occasion "Bob," from being more sensitive than the rest, fell from the vat, a height of some 10 feet, and in so doing dislocated the hip-joint. The other negroes occupied themselves in putting his leg in various comical positions, which would have been impossible but for the dislocation. This fact, to the negro mind so curious, with their excited state, and their inability to bring "Bob" to consciousness, caused them to be seized with a sudden sense of the ridiculous, which at all times, is peculiarly developed in the negro character; they, regardless of their situation, set up a shout of laughter —the well-known Yah-yah-yah—which led to their discovery. "Bob" was taken to the plantation hospital, where, on examination, I found the head of the femur thrown on the dorsum of the ilium; but as the muscles were all relaxed, no resistance was offered to the reduction of the dislocation. It was full half-an-hour before "Bob" returned to consciousness.*

Four years prior to this, the author had been rendered insensible by the inhalation of sulphuric ether, in Dr. Turner's lecture-room, University of London. The incident is recorded in the following letter:—

Huddersfield, Sept. 21st, 1868.

"DEAR SIR,—I perfectly well remember the *séance* held in the chemi-"cal lecture-room at University College, in the year 1835, for the purpose "of witnessing the inhalation of laughing gas, when, the supply of gas "being exhausted, Dr. Turner mentioned Sulphuric Ether as a substi-"tute, and one of the students volunteered to try it, and that he was "very ill in consequence. I cannot say that you were that student, "but I do very well remember your name as one of the prominent "members of Dr. Turner's class.

"Yours very truly,
"WM. J. CLARKE.

"DR. COLLYER, Bruges."

In 1842 and 1843, when repeating the feats of the Egyptian magicians in Boston, Philadelphia, and other places, amongst other substances I gave *Sulphuric Ether*. Nor does this depend on my assertion, for in a work published in Boston in April, 1843,—"The History and Philosophy of Animal Magnetism," at pp. 21 and 22, it is stated *Dr. Collyer caused the subjects to inhale the most powerful Ether*" (Sulphuric Ether).

The writer of this pamphlet has made a mistake, for he conveys a confused idea, that the persons in the mesmeric state were caused to inhale ether. He meant to say, the persons, who were my subjects, were caused to inhale powerful ether, otherwise the sentence is inconsistent, as persons in the *nervous congestive state* could not be made to inhale ether. In any case, it *proves the employment in public of Sulphuric Ether* in 1842 and 1843.

The publication of *Psychography* in Philadelphia, May, 1843, puts this matter beyond all question, for at pp. 26, 27, 28, 30, 32, 35, and 36,

---

* "The alcohols are strictly anæsthetics, and indeed the first published case of surgical operation under anæsthetic sleep was performed by Dr. Collyer, on a person who had been rendered insensible by breathing the fumes of alcohol."— Report read at the British Association of 1869, "On the Action of the Methyl and allied series," by Benj. W. Richardson, M.A., M.D., F.R.S.

ANÆSTHESIA. 7

I distinctly declare, that the unconscious or nervous congestive condition is induced by the *inhalation of narcotic and stimulating vapours*, and that the condition thus induced is not only *identical* with that produced by mesmerism, but also by mental excitement accompanied by muscular action, by steadily gazing on a fixed point for a length of time, natural fatigue, &c., &c.

The exact words published in the *Liverpool Mail*, Oct. 14th, 1843:—
"The topic for consideration was *Nervous Congestion*, or the accu-
"mulation of the nervous fluid in the great centres of the brain. This,
"the lecturer contended, explained that particular condition induced
"by fixing the eye on any given object, called by Mr. Braid the hyp
"notic state. This is now practised by the Hindoo Fakirs, and may be
"traced as early as the twelfth and thirteenth centuries, amongst the
"monks of Mount Tabor, the Kermalites, who fix themselves in one
"position, until they see the *light of faith*, being at the time unconscious
"of external things. Dr. Collyer proved that the brain distributed its
"resident principle to all the nerves of sense, and directly that commu-
"nication was cut off, the sleeping or the congestive state was always
"induced. This may be brought about: FIRST, by natural fatigue:
"SECOND, by the transmission of the nervous principle of a second per-
"son: THIRD, by concentration of the mind on any subject, accom-
"panied by muscular action: FOURTH, by steadily gazing on any
"object: FIFTH, BY INHALING NARCOTIC FUMES. ALL THESE PRODUCED THE
"SAME STATE OF BRAIN, &c. *From want of space* we are prevented
"giving the detail of this philosophical lecture."

All these modes of bringing about a state of unconsciousness or nervous congestion, "*produced the same state of brain.*"

It is impossible to lay too great stress on this publication of October, 1843, as it demonstrates conclusively that the unconscious state was produced by the inhalation of narcotic and stimulating vapours. The lectures I delivered included the whole philosophy of unconsciousness produced by inhalation, the condition of coma, somnambulism, trance, epileptic and hysterical coma.

Boston Daily Ledger, April 15th, 1842:—
"Those who had the pleasure of hearing Dr. Collyer on Tuesday
"evening will rememember, that he made some explanation of the ner-
"vous fluid, which produced the congestive state of the brain. He
"remarked that it was expended by the muscles, and its exhaustion
"rendered sleep necessary after the labours of the day, in order to collect
"a fresh supply. He also mentioned the fact, that, when the brain is
"*actively* employed, the communication with the body by means of the

"nerves ceases, so that the person is *insensible* to injuries received.
" He illustrated the Roman, who allowed his hand to be burnt off, to
" show the enemies of his country what the Romans could bear; the
" Christian martyrs under excitement; the dervishes and fakirs of Hin-
"dostan; and the soldiers, who in the heat of battle receive wounds,
" being unconscious of the pain, until the excitement of the battle
" had passed. Baron Larrey, the surgeon of Napoleon, gives instances
"in corroboration of this fact, that during EXCITEMENT SURGICAL
" OPERATIONS WERE BORNE WITHOUT APPARENT PAIN."

The following is from my Work published May, 1843, p. 36:—

" I had prepared by the magician's direction some frankincense and
" coriander seeds; a chafing-dish, *with some live coals* in it. These were
" now brought into the room, together with the boy who was to be em-
"ployed; he had been called in by my desire from amongst other boys
" in the street, returning from a manufactory, and was about eight
" or nine years of age.

" In reply to my inquiry respecting the person who could see in the
" *magic mirror of ink*, the magician said, they were: *a boy* not arrived
" *at puberty, a virgin*, a black female slave, and a *pregnant woman.*

"The chafing-dish was placed before him and the boy; the latter
" was placed on a seat. The magician now addressed my servant to
" put some frankincense and coriander seeds into the chafing-dish,
" *then taking hold* of the boy's right hand, he drew in the palm of it a
" magic square: in the centre he poured a little ink and desired the boy
" to look into it and tell him if he could see his face reflected in it; the boy
" replied that he saw his face clearly; the magician, *holding the boy's*
" *hand all the while*, told him to look silently into the ink and *not*
" to *raise his head*. He then took one of the strips of paper inscribed
" with the forms of invocation, and dropped it into the *chafing-dish*
" upon the burning coals and perfumes, which had ALREADY FILLED
" THE ROOM WITH THEIR SMOKE; and as he did this he commenced
" indistinct mutterings of words, which he continued during the whole
" process, &c., &c.

" While this was going on, the magician put the second and third
" of the small strips of paper, upon which the forms of invocation were
" written, into the chafing-dish, *fresh frankincense and coriander*
" *seeds* being repeatedly added, UNTIL THE FUMES BECAME PAINFUL
" TO THE EYES.

" The object of placing the boy near the window was evidently for
" him *to inhale* the fumes, it being the only window open, the vapours
" would naturally be directed to that point.

ANÆSTHESIA.

"A pure seer, to wit, a maiden's or a boy's eye was required. These are constitutionally more susceptible to the influence of the "'*Narcotic and Stimulating Vapours.*' I find that, with very little trouble, they are subdued by the nervous agency, whereas stronger persons, as men and old women, are very hard to be affected."

The only difference made by me, was in the addition of *poppy* (for which I substituted the bowl of molasses), and the vapour from alcohol, with which was sometimes mixed ether. In many places, I was forced to give my lectures without the experiments, from the fact of the fumes being painful to the audience.

The reader must take all the extracts in connexion with the surgical operations constantly performed by me in public, during the anæsthetic state induced by mesmerism.

The *Boston Daily Ledger* of May 28th, 1842, is as follows:—

"Dr. Collyer's experiments were very successful. He first mesmerized "Frederick—when he showed the reality of his unconscious state by "exciting and depressing his pulse at pleasure (by acting on the heart).

"A young lady was mesmerized for the purpose of having a tooth "extracted; the tooth was examined by several physicians, amongst "whom was Dr. Sampson, of Brewster, one of the Counsellors of the "Massachusetts Medical Society; they pronounced the tooth to be "decayed, but firm in the head. Dr. Kimball, who had consented to "extract it, then applied his instrument, but the tooth was so much "decayed that it crumbled and broke, but was extracted in a second "trial. During all this time those who stood near declared that they "did not observe the least change of countenance in the young lady."

One of the persons present was the self-same Wm. T. G. Morton who subsequently, in 1846—four years after—claimed, in company with Dr. Charles T. Jackson, to be the discoverer of ether inhalation.

But the most important published document is from the *Providence Evening Chronicle* of March 17th, 1843:—

"The lecture of Dr. Collyer, at Westminster Hall, last evening, was "on the Philosophy of the Nervous Force. Man must be called an "electrical machine—indeed he was so, most truly; he was governed "by its laws, and exhibited most of the phenomena connected with that "fluid. Magnetic sleep was a congestion of the brain produced by the "transmission of the nervous force from one person to another. To "illustrate this, in brain fever, where there is an over action of that "part of the body, we find the patient has cold hands and feet; here "is a withdrawal from those parts of the nervous force to supply this "extra action of the brain. *He noticed the beautiful action of the lungs*

"*in this connexion.* Monotony would produce sleep on the most irri-
"table when all opiates fail; waking was only the result of the constant
"stimulus of the variety which meets our gaze. Printers often experi-
"enced this in a blurred sheet, or a double impression on the same
"sheet. By looking at any object for a long time, a dimness would
"come over the eyes, languor, &c.: in fact, all the approaching attri-
"butes of sleep or a congestion of the brain, as in common sleep or
"the mesmeric sleep, would be produced. He further alluded to the
"action of the nervous force as connected with the brain. Men in
"strife received *bruises and wounds*, and are not sensible of the fact at
"the time, in consequence of the great excitement of the brain pro-
"ducing a deadness of the outer surface: or, in other words, a with-
"drawal of the nervous force to supply the increased action of the
"central portions of the brain. Any excitement would produce the
"same result; as we see in the Hindoo widow, in the Indian of the
"forest, who seems at times wholly indifferent to pain, and will bear
"the most apparently excruciating torture without a murmur. In
"cases of religious excitement the same action is made manifest.
"Persons under this religious frenzy do what, under ordinary circum-
"stances, they could not do, until at length the brain becomes ex-
"hausted, and the subject falls into a swoon, in which they lie for
"hours and even days. By exciting a person's vanity we have *the same*
"result; SURGICAL OPERATIONS have been performed, where the patient
"has borne the pain with the greatest fortitude, when his feelings have
"been appealed to. A Roman general once boasted of the great power
"of the Romans to bear pain, and plunged his arm into the fire until
"it dropped off. In a condition where there is an equilibrium of the
"system, the sting of a mosquito will almost drive one mad. Dr.
"Collyer gave the statement of a celebrated French surgeon (Baron
"Larrey), who accompanied Napoleon in all his campaigns, to substan-
"tiate his position. This *surgeon stated that operations* were always
"better borne by the soldiers, if performed immediately after an en-
"gagement, while *the excitement was on*, than if performed at a later
"period."

In April, 1843, the writer gave a course of lectures in the Museum lecture-room, Philadelphia. Those on the feats of the Egyptian magicians necessitated the inhalation of the narcotic and stimulating vapours. It was at this period, that Dr. Hare, Professor of Chemistry in the University of Pennsylvania, gave me his valuable aid, and the most powerful electro-magnetic battery was applied to the persons rendered unconscious, nervo-congestive state, by the inhalation of narcotic and stimulating vapours. At one of these lectures, a Miss Allen inhaled the fumes of powdered poppy-heads, coriander, and olibanum, to which was added the vapour from rectified spirits of wine (alcohol). She was soon rendered unconscious, and during that state had a tooth extracted—painlessly. It was *at this time* that I wrote the passage in *Psychography* :—"The inhalation of narcotic and *stimu-* "*lating* vapours produces a state of insensibility (anæsthetic state) "identical with that produced by the various other methods of bringing "about 'the same state of brain.'"

I also extract from the *Liverpool Standard*, October 17th, 1843, a partial report of one of *my lectures* :—

"Fakirs *mesmerized* by inhaling narcotic fumes, *narcotizing;* after "excitement in battle, MESMERIC COLLAPSE—likewise in drunkenness, "wounds not felt, because nervous force is taken away by mental excite- "ment;—Suttee, Hindoo Widow when burnt on the funeral pile of "her husband, does not feel, because *excited*, explains Scævola's case "of arm thrust into the fire under stimulus of mind, &c. &c. Electricity "is vitalized by the lungs and assimilated."

The substances which I used to *narcotize* were: powdered poppy-seeds, coriander, olibanum, myrrh, &c. These, when powdered and mixed, were thrown on live charcoal, and a funnel was placed on the chafing-dish; these fumes were inhaled, and often produced the most profound anæsthetic state in one or two minutes. I used, on some occasions, the vapour from rectified spirit of wine, boiling the same in an oil flask, which was mixed with the narcotic fumes.

In Boston (1842) I repeated the experiments of the Egyptian magicians, before audiences from 1000 to 1500 persons, producing all the conditions of the anæsthetic state, by the inhalation of these narcotic and stimulating vapours.

The constant and persistent object was the application of the anæsthetic state to surgical operations, *no matter how the unconscious or insensible state was induced*. This fact is *most important*, in showing that Dr. Collyer did *not* confine the surgical application of anæsthesia to the so-called mesmeric state.

The *Liverpool Standard*, October 17th, 1843, says :—"To prove that "mental hallucination could be induced by the operator, he took a "young woman, only *semi-mesmerized* (waking-state), and placed a jug "in her hands, which she recognised to be *a pig*. By a pass of his "hand, she began to stroke it as a pet cat, which she declared was "such; and the influence being removed, her own surprise at her mis- "take was pictured by a look and expression of shame before the large

"audience, which could not be feigned. Again her mind was influ-
"enced, and she saw a large fish at her side, from which she endeavoured
"to escape with every gesture of horror, until the influence was re-
"moved. A young man and young woman, *both perfect strangers* to
"Dr. Collyer, were placed in a rigid or cataleptic condition of the
"muscles (though otherwise perfectly awake). Dr. Collyer stated that
"he knew of TWO OPERATIONS having been performed in America during
"this state—viz., extirpation of CANCER FROM THE FOOT, and ADJUST-
"MENT OF A COMPOUND FRACTURE OF THE FORE-ARM. In the latter
"case a portion of bone was removed, in order to set the limb (gene-
"rally a painful operation), and yet the patient *was insensible*."

The function of the lungs is specially called into requisition, when narcotic and stimulating vapours are inhaled. In the abnormal respiratory condition they supply the brain and nervous system with nervo-vital fluid. The following, published in February, 1844, in the *Phrenological Journal*, will explain my views at that date :—

THE LUNGS A GALVANIC OR NERVO-ELECTRIC BATTERY.

To the Editor of the People's Phrenological Journal.

"DEAR SIR,—In many of the late numbers of your periodical, I
"observe, that a *recent* (?) discovery has been made relative to the
"functions of the lungs. In November last, during my sojourn in
"London, handbills were circulated of the following description : '*A new
"discovery*, the lungs a galvanic battery ! C. B. Keenan, Esq., M.D.,
"will give two lectures at the Parthenium, in which he will prove that
"the lungs are especially a galvanic battery, &c.' This bill, had its
"claim been less startling, would not have attracted my attention.

"It is at all times an unpleasant task, to show that an individual
"has been anticipated, by years, in the public advocacy of a doctrine
"in which he supposes himself the discoverer. Dr. Keenan has only
"to refer to *printed* works to *discover* that the author broached the
"selfsame ideas, without any modification. In the year 1840, I ad-
"vanced the doctrine, that the lungs, at every inspiration, send elec-
"tricity to the brain; which having been assimilated by the lungs to
"subserve the purposes of life, I called the nervo-electric principle or
"fluid. In fact, this theory involved two hours' lecture. The same I
"again advanced in the spring of 1841, in Boston, 1842, in Montreal,
"Quebec, Toronto; in 1843, the identical words were pronounced in
"Liverpool, to which a large majority of the medical gentlemen will
"bear witness. Again, I find that a pupil of mine, the Rev. J. B.
"Dodds, in a pamphlet published in January, 1843, uses these words

ANÆSTHESIA. 13

"at page 16, 'We thus perceive that the nervo-vital fluid is manufac-
"tured out of electricity taken into the lungs at every inspiration.'
"Again, at p. 20: 'Hence, I have clearly proved that the nervo-vital
"fluid, secreted by the brain, is of a *galvanic* nature, and is manufac-
"tured from electricity which we breathe into the *lungs* at every
"inspiration we take.'*

"I am not desirous of making any unnecessary comments on the
"above. But it requires no ghost from the grave to convince us, that
"Dr. Keenan has not made *a new discovery*, in stating that the lungs
"generate nervous power. The same ideas have been advocated long
"before either of us were born.

"Should the parties still persist in the claim to originality, I will,
"on my visit to London, show you chapter and verse in proof to the
"contrary.
"Yours respectfully,
"ROBERT H. COLLYER, M.D.
"Liverpool, January 27th, 1844."

When narcotic and stimulating vapours are inhaled, the ordinary functions are so much increased as to produce *nervous congestion*, an unconscious or anæsthetic state. For it is proved, that during the sleep and insensibility produced by artificial means, the brain is not supplied with blood to the same extent as during its activity in the waking state. I particularly mention this, as the writer in the *Lancet* has entirely misrepresented my ideas as regards *nervous congestion* of the brain.

At this epoch (1845), Dr. Esdaile, in Calcutta, was prosecuting a series of experiments, which for boldness and originality are not surpassed in the history of surgery; these surgical operations attracted so much attention, that the Deputy-Governor of Bengal appointed a committee composed of Dr. Atkinson, Inspector-General of Hospitals, Dr. O'Shaughnessy, Dr. Stewart, Presidency Surgeon of Bengal, including many other men of eminence, who reported on the surgical operations performed under their own observation. Some of the results were indefinite, whilst others were most successful.

During the nervous congestive state induced, one man, Sept. 17th, 1846, had a thigh amputated by the double-flap operation, seven arteries being secured, lasting fifteen minutes, during the whole time not the slightest movement or manifestation of sensibility was exhibited. In another case—hypertrophy of the scrotum—the tumour,

---
* *Vide* lecture reported in the *Liverpool Standard*, October, 1813.—"He described the nervo-vital power as electricity vitalized by assimilation in the lungs."

weighing 16¼ lbs., was removed without pain. In a third case, the stupor induced by Dr. Esdaile was so profound that Dr. Stewart believed the patient had drugged himself with Indian hemp, "bang;" at the request of the committee he was awakened, when it was found the suspicion was unfounded. In a fourth case, Dr. Esdaile removed from a Hindoo, twenty-seven years of age, a scrotal tumour, which measured seven feet in circumference and two feet round its neck; the tumour was as large as the body of the man, half an hour after it was removed, was found to weigh 103 lbs. This wonderful operation was performed without the least evidence of pain or consciousness; the time occupied in the operation was six minutes, including the application of ligatures to the spermatic and other arteries. It must be remembered, that this anæsthetic state was produced without inhalation, but by producing a nervous congestive state of the brain by an extra supply of nervous fluid from a second person.—*Vide* Appendix; *Lancet's* "History of Anæsthetic Discovery."

In the summer of 1846 I returned to Europe and visited the Island of Jersey, where I practised my profession as a physician, and occasionally gave public lectures. In one of these, December 10th, 1846, I gave a *resumé* of the anæsthetic discovery. This was SIX DAYS prior to the arrival of the Cunard steamer *Acadia*, which brought the news of the *alleged* discovery of Wm. T. G. Morton of September 30th, 1846. The following attestation was voluntarily given me:—

"St. Heliers, Jersey, Jan. 2nd, 1847.

" We, the undersigned, were present at a lecture delivered by Dr. "Collyer on the evening of December 10th, 1846, in this town. We " distinctly heard him state, that he had frequently, by the inhalation " of narcotic and stimulating vapours, brought about a state of uncon- " sciousness like that produced by the mesmeric passes, and that " during that state all kinds of surgical operations could be performed " without pain to the patient.

"(Signed) A. J. Le Cras.   A. J. Howard.
           G. G. Bowring.   G. G. Irwin.
           A. Le Bas.   Fred. M. Young.
           B. Thompson.   A. W. Alderson.
           J. Deslandes.   H. Alderson.
           S. Thompson.   Herbert A. Gray.
           H. Thompson.   J. De la Taste.
           Col. J. C. J. Davidson. J. H. Fergerson.
           M. J. Preshaw, *Surgeon*. M. W. Holloway."

ANÆSTHESIA. 15

The value of the above is incontestible, as showing, that I constantly claimed the production of the anæsthetic state by the inhalation of narcotic and stimulating vapours,—the same as I had published in *Psychography* in May, 1843, and also in the *Liverpool Mail* of October, 1843.

In March, 1847, or seven months prior to the first use of Chloroform by Dr. James Simpson of Edinburgh, these words are used by me in the London *Critic:*—

"The lungs are the manufacturing organs of the system; they supply the wasted powers, their functions being particularly in action during sleep; whenever any *stimulating vapour* is applied to them, their productive function is much increased. This is the case on the inhalation of Ether and protoxide of nitrogen *or any other stimulating vapour.*"

This latter expression is of major importance at this date (1871), as showing, that *my experiments* were not confined to any special anæsthetic, as many substances had been already tried by me. At this moment the list of substances which, when inhaled, produce insensible unconsciousness, (anæsthesia) may be stated as not less than 25 in number, and without doubt, experience will discover as many more.

It is historically significant, that in 1842, 1843, and 1844, I should have published these two most important facts, which the investigation of the profession should have since discovered *to be correct.* 1st. That the anæsthetic state is a *nervous congestion* of the brain in contradistinction to an increased flow of blood to that organ. 2nd. That any stimulating vapour, when inhaled, produces the anæsthetic state.

No one could now have the hardihood to deny this, as the original publications exist.

On concluding this chapter the reader must refer to the Appendix, where will be found the copy of certificates of copyright of *Psychography*, the original copy of which still exists; also the copy of the official Mexican documents, as to the lost papers and diplomas, in 1849.

CHAPTER II.

CONTENDING CLAIMS OF HORACE WELLS, WM. T. G. MORTON, AND DR. CHARLES T. JACKSON.

THE moment the news arrived in the Isle of Jersey, I addressed to the *Jersey Times*, the London *Medical Times*, London *Critic*, London *Morning Chronicle, Lancet, &c. &c.*

PAINLESS SURGICAL OPERATIONS PRODUCED BY INHALATION.

To the Editor of the Medical Times.

"SIR,—Monopoly is opposed to the spirit of the age, more particu-
"larly with a subject, the application of which must tend to the
"alleviation of much human suffering. As I can without doubt prove
"that, prior to the arrival of the *Acadia* steamer in Liverpool on the
"16th of December last, at a public lecture on the 10th of the same
"month, I did declare that I had oftentimes produced unconsciousness
"by the *inhalation* of '*Narcotic* and Stimulating Vapours,' so that
"*surgical operations* might be performed without pain to the patient
"during that condition,—*I urge this claim now in consequence of* AN
"ADVERTISEMENT THAT THE USE OF INHALATION FOR SURGICAL OPERATIONS
"WAS BEING PATENTED. This is indeed most preposterous! I, as the
"rightful claimant, NOW GIVE IT *cheerfully* and *freely* to all who desire
"to use it. In the year 1842 I tried the experiment on more than
"twenty persons: in fine, the unconscious state lasted from half an hour
"to two hours,* whereas the recent experiments in America do not pro-
"duce unconsciousness for a longer period than two to five minutes.
"I would not have it supposed that mesmerism is in any degree inter-
"fered with in consequence of the production of unconsciousness by
"inhalation. In the list of nervous diseases—neuralgia, paralysis,
"headaches, epilepsy, palsy, &c.—mesmerism must be resorted to.
"Moreover, the whole credit of inhalation 'is due to mesmerism,' and
"the state induced is, in every way, a similar one. In the year 1843,
"I published a Work simultaneously in Philadelphia, New York, and

---

* That is, I could not restore the patient to a perfect state of consciousness in some cases under two hours; in one instance, the nervous congestive state induced was so deep, that I was fearful of a fatal result.

"Boston, wherein, at pages 26, 27, and 28, I distinctly and unequi-vocally declare, that UNCONSCIOUSNESS CAN BE PRODUCED BY THE INHA-LATION OF NARCOTIC AND STIMULATING VAPOURS.

"More than a thousand copies were sold, and my experiments by *inhalation* were the topic of conversation from one end of the United States to the other. There was hardly an editor who had not a joke on the 'bowl of molasses experiment,' as it was called at the time. I have fortunately several copies with me. Dr. Elliotson, in the third number of the *Zoist*, refers to it.

"I know, then, that you will render me every facility of vindicating that which is most dear to every man—REPUTATION—and the priority of having produced a condition, whose application must tend to the alleviation of much human suffering.

"I am, yours respectfully,
"ROBERT H. COLLYER, M.D.
"St. Heliers, Jersey, January 2nd, 1847."

Even at this period, I had never heard of Horace Wells, who was in Paris engaged in the purchase of pictures, which was his business, he having entirely abandoned all idea of using anæsthetic agents, since his first discomfiture in Boston. On the 11th of February, 1847, Mr. Wells wrote a letter, which was published in *Galignani's Messenger*, which will be found in the Appendix. I am reluctantly obliged to state, that it is an entire misrepresentation of the facts, which will be dwelt on hereafter.

It seems that in December, 1844, Mr. J. Q. Coulton visited Hartford, Connecticut, for the purpose of exhibiting the effects of protoxide of nitrogen, or laughing gas.* A Mr. Cooley inhaled the gas, which caused him to dance, and resort to other muscular exercises; he in so doing severely contused his ankles, so much so, that blood flowed freely from the wounds. He was unconscious of having received any injury at the time.† Mr. Horace Wells,‡ dentist, being one of the audience, took

---

* There were many persons entirely *ignorant* of chemistry, who travelled in various parts of the United States, administering the laughing gas. A Mr. Preston, of New York, in 1841 made this his business.

† *Vide* my lecture delivered in Providence, March 16th, 1843:—"Men in strife receive bruises and wounds, and are not sensible of the fact at the time, in con-sequence of the excitement of brain producing a deadness of the outer surface, or, in other words, a withdrawal of the nervous force, to supply the increased action of the central portions of the brain. Any excitement would produce the same results," &c.

‡ Neither Mr. Wells nor Morton had received a medical education, and were en-tirely ignorant of physiology.

notice of the circumstance that Mr. Cooley had experienced no pain, and suggested to him the idea, that teeth might be extracted during *the excitement* caused by inhaling the nitrous oxide gas. Mr. Wells the next day had a tooth extracted from his own head.

This is Mr. Coulton's account of the transaction. As he it was who administered the gas, no doubt it may be relied on as perfectly correct, but it is diametrically opposed to the account published by Wells himself in *Galignani's Messenger* in February, 1847, but which agrees with the published statement of Dr. Ellsworth, in the *Boston Medical and Surgical Journal* of December 16th, 1846, and that of Dr. Marcy, December 30th, 1846. Had not these gentlemen, in order to advance themselves, published these contradictory letters, Mr. Wells never would have sent this unfortunate letter to *Galignani's Messenger*, wherein he says:—
" Reasoning from analogy, I was led to believe that surgical operations
" might be performed without pain, by the fact, that an individual when
" much excited, &c." *Vide* Letter in Appendix.

Of course, no one can know who has not investigated the matter how this is at variance with the facts. It is most important, as showing a total absence of memory on the part of Wells. He entirely ignores having derived the idea from Mr. Coulton's exhibition of the gas, and *the wounding of Mr. Cooley.* Mr.—*now* Dr. G. Q. Coulton—*thought so little of it* at the time of Mr. Wells's experiments, that he did not adopt it until the year 1863, or 19 years subsequently !

In the following month (January, 1845), Wells visited Boston, for the purpose of introducing the practice of inhalation. He first called on Mr. Wm. T. G. Morton, *his former partner* in the practice of dentistry. Mr. Morton, in his account of this interview, which he sent to the French Academy of Science, July 13th, 1847, corroborates what Mr. Wells himself stated, and there seems little doubt but that it is substantially correct.

Mr. Morton says, " In the course of the winter of 1844 and 1845, Mr.
" Horace Wells, of Hartford, Connecticut, dentist, previously my
" partner, called on me in Boston. He asked me to aid him in finding
" an occasion to administer the nitrous oxide gas, which he said
" destroyed, or at least relieved very much, the pain of surgical opera-
" tions. I readily consented, and presented him to Dr. Hayward, an
" eminent surgeon, who was perfectly willing to make the experiment ;
" but as the operation could not take place for two or three days, we did
" not wait for that occasion, and we went to Dr. Warren, whom we found
" about to deliver his course of lectures. He told us his students would
" be willing to inhale the gas in the evening, for a change and amuse-

"ment; he asked them to meet us in the evening at the college. In "the evening Mr. Wells and myself went to the lecture-room. I brought "my dental instruments, and Mr. Wells administered the gas for the "extraction of a tooth, but the patient cried out from the pain pro- "duced,* and the students *laughed and hissed*. The *séance* then ended, "and we found that we had rendered ourselves ridiculous. I did not "see Mr. Wells again, except early next morning, when he returned my "instruments. He then returned to Hartford.

"In July following (1845) I went to Hartford, and devoted some "time with Mr. Wells in the regulation of our accounts of a former "partnership. He (Mr. Wells) had abandoned his profession as dentist, "and was occupied in the direction of an Exhibition of Birds: this, he "said, was much better for his health. I went with him to the office "of Dr. Riggs, where we talked of the gas. I asked him to give me "a little, but he made me understand that he had abandoned his "experiments, thinking them of no practical value."

The reader must carefully compare this account with the following letter, in reply to Mr. Morton, dated October 20th, 1846. It will be seen that, from December to January, Mr. Wells made a few desultory, unmethodical trials with the nitrous oxide gas; he never produced *narcosis*, or a state of *unconsciousness;* for, as Dr. Ellsworth says, "the patients appeared merry during the operation." Had Mr. Wells been an educated man, had he understood the anatomy and physiology of the human economy, he would have carried his experiments to a stage of complete coma; had he done so, the *apparent failure* before Dr. Warren's class would not have taken place.

The following letters, which passed between Morton and Wells, exhibit their limited knowledge on the subject of anæsthesia, at the time.

"Boston, October 19th, 1846.
"FRIEND WELLS,
"DEAR SIR,—I write to inform you, that I have discovered *a* "*preparation,* by inhaling which a person is thrown into a sound sleep. "The time required to produce sleep is only a few moments, and the "time in which persons remain asleep can be regulated at pleasure; "while in this state the severest surgical operations may be per- "formed, the patient not experiencing the slightest pain. I have "*patented* it, and am now about sending out agents to dispose of the

---

* Probably no pain was experienced. Patients under the influence of anæsthetics continually make demonstrations, as if they suffered pain; but, on coming to consciousness, declare that they have experienced none.

" right to use it. I will dispose of the right to an individual to use it
" in his practice alone, or for a town, country, or state. My object in
" writing to you is, to know if you would like to visit New York, and
" other cities, to dispose of rights in shares. I have used *the compound*
" in more than one hundred and sixty cases in extracting teeth, and I
" have been invited to administer it to patients in the Massachusetts
" General Hospital, and have succeeded in every case.
" Respectfully yours,
" WM. T. G. MORTON."

To which Mr. Wells replies:—

" Hartford, October 20th, 1846.
" DR. MORTON,
" DEAR SIR,—Your letter dated yesterday is just received, and I
" hasten to answer it, for I fear you will adopt a method of disposing
" of your rights, which will defeat your object. Before you make any
" arrangement whatever, I wish to see you. I think I will be in
" Boston next week, probably Monday night. *If the operation of*
" *administering the gas is not attended with too much trouble, and will*
" *produce the effects you state*, it will be undoubtedly a fortune to you,
" provided it is rightly managed.
" Yours in haste,
" H. WELLS."

The italics are mine. "If the operation of administering *the gas*
" is not attended with too much trouble, and produces the effects you
" state."

It is evident, that Mr. Wells, at this date, had never administered
sulphuric ether, nor had he ever produced a state of coma or narcosis.
How does he reconcile this letter with that published in *Galignani's
Messenger*, wherein, he says:—" I have administered nitrous oxide gas
" and the vapour of ether to about fifty persons ; my operations having
" been limited to this small number, in consequence of a protracted
" illness, which immediately ensued on my return from Boston, in
" January, 1845. Mr. Wells in his *Galignani* letter ignores, or forgets
" the *Coulton exhibition*, when Mr. Cooley wounded his ankles, but
" says, '*Reasoning from analogy, I was led to believe that surgical
" operations might be performed, &c.*'" *Vide* Letter in Appendix.

Had Mr. Wells reasoned the matter, and made experiments as the
result of that reasoning; he never would have abandoned the subject
because of discomfiture or *partial* success in Boston. The truth is,

Mr. Wells never dreamt of producing a state of *unconsciousness, and never thought* of rendering surgical operations painless, until he saw the exhibition of nitrous oxide in December, 1844, by Mr. Coulton. Nor did he ever, at any time, up to writing the letter to *Galignani*, administer ether vapour. His letter to Mr. Morton conclusively proves this fact. That Mr. Morton and Wells were on the best terms, their letters demonstrate, and as they were partners, it is not likely that, had Mr. Wells administered *the ether* in December, 1844, and January, 1845—as he says—Mr. Morton would have been ignorant of its use in September, 1846, when he asked Dr. Jackson where it could be obtained, *and what kind of looking stuff it was!*

The moment Morton took out the patent, and the use of sulphuric ether became known, two persons made themselves conspicuously prominent. I refer to Drs. Ellsworth and Marcy. These gentlemen wrote letters to the leading journals, claiming for themselves the *priority*, the one as having suggested *the use of ether*, the other as being the first to *publish*.

Both hailing from Hartford, Wells was a most convenient and pliable instrument; he exactly suited their purpose. It was the extravagant assertions published by these gentlemen which induced Mr. Wells to publish *the Galignani letter*.

Wells returned to New York, where, in the autumn of 1847, I met him, quite accidentally, in an oyster saloon. We had a long conversation relative to his connexion with Morton, and the administration of protoxide of nitrogen gas; he at that time did not think the production of unconsciousness necessary, or even possible. Mr. Wells acknowledged having attended my lectures in 1842 and 1843 in Boston, and also having read my work published in 1843.

Dr. Henry Bennet communicated to the *Lancet* in March 1847, that Mr. Wells had called on him ; he says—

"If the discovery should eventually prove as great a boon to "humanity as many of the most eminent men in the profession believe "it will, it is very desirable that we should know *to whom* our gratitude "is really due. I am therefore, personally, most happy to have it in "my power to communicate the following documents to you. They will "tend to dispel the kind of mystery that has hitherto seemed to conceal "the origin, in America, of painless operations. I may add that Mr. "Wells has promised to forward me, on his arrival in America, other "documents substantiating his claims, which I will not fail to com-"municate as soon as received."

The documents referred to by Dr. Bennet are the Galignani letters, and two letters written by Drs. Marcy and Ellsworth. *Vide* Appendix, pages 121, 127, 128.

It will be seen that Mr. Wells did not fulfil his promise in furnishing further proof, in fine, there was none to communicate.

On Wells's return to America, in April 1847, he put himself in communication with Drs. Marcy and Ellsworth. Three cases are reported in the *Boston Medical and Surgical Journal*, where the nitrous oxide gas was administered by Mr. Wells, and Dr. Marcy operated in the removal of a large scirrhous testicle. This operation was performed at Hartford, August 17th, 1847, and lasted fifteen minutes—so says Dr. Marcy. The next case is the amputation of a thigh in Hartford, by Dr. Ellsworth, the nitrous oxide gas having been administered by Mr. Wells. Dr. Hall, who sent the report to the *Medical Journal*, January 1st, 1848, *makes use of this singular expression*—" Mr. Wells gave the patient the gas a second time, *in order to allow a large nerve to be divided.*"

On the 4th of January, 1848, Bristol, Connecticut, a tumour was removed by Dr. S. B. Beresford, the patient having inhaled the gas administered by Wells. He, however, failed entirely in the *New York Hospitals*, the ether being preferred.

In consequence of the melancholy and untimely death of Horace Wells in New York, January 24th, 1848, the further use of nitrous oxide gas as an anæsthetic, was postponed, and remained unheeded until 1863, when Dr. G. Q. Coulton returned to its use. It is through the perseverance of this gentleman, that the world is indebted to its general adoption in minor surgical operations.

It is here shown, that Mr. Wells only returned to the use of nitrous oxide after Morton's successful experiments on the 30th September, 1846. It is perfectly true, as Colonel Bissell, chairman of the Select Committee appointed by Congress, to investigate the anæsthetic claims, says in his report—" that Wells had totally *abandoned* the use of nitrous oxide—that is, from January 1845, to August 1847."

There is not the least proof that *unconsciousness* was ever produced, nor is it essential in the production of insensibility. Had, however, Wells known that unconsciousness could have been produced by the inhalation he would not have been subjected to the mortifications he had to submit to, from the supposed failure of the nitrous oxide, in *not* producing *insensibility*.

The whole controversy of Wells, Morton, and their friends, verifies the French adage—

"Ils mentent comme des arracheurs des dents."

CHAPTER III.

CONTENDING CLAIMS OF WM. T. G. MORTON AND DR. CHARLES T. JACKSON.

NEARLY two years had passed since the experiment of Horace Wells on himself with nitrous oxide gas, to produce insensibility, so as to have the tooth extracted by Dr. Riggs: yet no one seemed to heed the experiment. We are brought to another stage, where Mr. Wm. T. G. Morton plays the most prominent part.

Dr. Charles T. Jackson became, by mere accident, associated with Morton. This is the language used by the former when writing of the latter, March, 1847:—"*He is profoundly ignorant and utterly incapable* "*of scientific investigation.* He came to me for the loan of a gas bag, "for the administration of atmospheric air, *or something else*, to a lady, "in order to calm her fears relative to the extraction of a tooth. I "replied," says Dr. Jackson, "that the apparatus was in the laboratory, "and the obtaining it was attended with some trouble."*

Dr. Morton then replied: "I wish to act on her imagination, after "the manner related of what took place on a criminal condemned to "death; whose eyes were bandaged, when a small current of warm "water was allowed to run as if from an orifice of the veins."

Dr. Jackson said: "This trial will fail, and you will be rendered "ridiculous, and considered a greater humbug than Wells with his "nitrous oxide."†

Up to this moment both Morton and Jackson agree; and now comes the most improbable part of Dr. Jackson's statement. This was made only on the 1st of March, 1847! He (Jackson) says:—"I instigated "the use of ether to cause the lady *to sleep*, and then you can extract "her tooth, and she cannot defend herself, nor make any resistance "to your operation." Dr. Jackson seems to forget what he swore to before R. H. Eddy, Justice of the Peace, October 27th, 1846—namely,

---

* I cannot conceive the trouble of obtaining *a small gas bag.*
† Both Dr. Jackson and Morton always ignored the anæsthetic properties of the nitrous oxide gas!

"that at this time neither Dr. Morton nor myself had any idea, that "any one had inhaled ether to abolish pain during a surgical opera- "tion." "It is reckless and heedless on the part of Morton to do as "he is doing; it is very likely to happen that he will kill some one." Had Dr. Jackson made the statement prior to Morton's extraction of Frost's tooth (September 30th, 1846), then his claim would have some weight, or probability of being founded in truth. As it is, I am forced to give the whole of the credit, such as it is, to Morton; *he took the responsibility.* It is certain that he had heard of sulphuric ether prior to his calling on Jackson, whom he desired to mislead by the invention of desiring to act on the imagination of the lady. All Morton *wanted, was the gas bag.* Dr. Jackson always repudiated the anæs- thetic properties of nitrous oxide, and in his pamphlet, *Etherization* (published in 1848), page 13, he says, "by oft-repeated experiments in "the inhalation of protoxide on myself and others in every possible "way, I soon became fully satisfied *that it possessed no anæsthetic "properties."* Will any one believe this *now,* in 1871?

Dr. Jackson, you have used a double-edged sword, which cuts both ways. If you were satisfied that nitrous oxide possessed no anæs- thetic properties, how is it that you pretend to have said to Morton, "*Give the lady ether:* it will send her to sleep"?

To the unprofessional reader. It must be remembered, that in the chemical lecture-room of the Medical Schools of Europe and America, ether as a substitute for nitrous oxide, has been used for the past 50 years, since Professor Faraday pointed out the analogous pro- perties of the two substances.

Wm. T. G. Morton's account seems, to the author, more consistent with truth. He says: "*Thinking the occasion a good one,* I said, with "all the indifference I could feign, '*Why cannot I give ether?*' 'You "can do so,' said he, and repeated to me that which he had already "told the students at Cambridge. He added, that the patient would be "dull and stupefied, that I could do all I wished; but that he would "be outside the affair, nor would he take any responsibility."

This statement at least coincides with the evidence of Messrs. Eddy. The most extraordinary part of the transaction on the part of Messrs. Morton and Jackson was, securing Letters Patent conjointly on the 27th of October, 1846, and causing advertisements for the sale of licences to appear in all the medical journals of England, America, and France. Morton says in his *memoire* to the Paris Academy of Science:—"I gave *gratuitously* my rights to all charitable institutions." Was this the fact? In his advertisement, he charges five guineas to charitable hospitals, infirmaries, and dispensaries. He also brought an action against the New York Eye Infirmary for infringement of his patent. This did not look like a gratuitous giving of his patent rights!

I must here correct an error which prevails to a great extent in Europe, of confounding Wm. T. G. Morton, the dentist of Boston, with the distinguished physiologist Dr. Samuel George Morton, Professor of Medicine, and late President of the Academy of Sciences, Philadelphia, Author of *Crania Americana*, &c. &c.

Drs. Jackson and Morton made oath conjointly on the 27th October, 1846, to wit—

"It has never, to our knowledge, been known until our discovery, "that the inhalation of vapours, particularly those of Sulphuric Ether, " would produce insensibility to pain, and we claim the application of " ether or the vapour thereof substantially as described."

How is it possible to reconcile this oath with Dr. Jackson's statement to Mr. Eddy?

"*Pecuniary sacrifices*"—are claimed by Morton. The pecuniary idea seems to have been the prevailing sentiment with Wells, Morton, and Jackson. Wells writes to Morton in October,1846,—"It will undoubtedly be a fortune to you, provided it is rightly managed." Dr. Jackson makes it a *sine quâ non* that he should receive 500 dollars in cash, besides 10 per cent on all the profits of the patent, and subsequently he demanded 25 per cent, which Morton refused. Dr. Jackson makes oath with Mr. Morton on the 27th of October, 1846, that they are conjoint discoverers of the ether inhalation process. On the 13th of November, Dr. Jackson writes the following letter to the Paris Academy of Science :—

"Boston, November 13th, 1846.

" I request to communicate, through your medium, to the Academy " of Science, a discovery which I have made, and which I believe im- " portant for the relief of suffering humanity, as well as of great value " to the surgical profession. *Five or six years ago*,* I noticed the pecu- "liar state of insensibility into which the nervous system is thrown by " the inhalation of pure Sulphuric Ether, which I respired abundantly, " first, by way of experiment, and afterwards when I had a severe " catarrh caused by the inhalation of chlorine gas. I have lately made a " useful application of this fact by persuading a dentist of this city to

---

* *Most indefinite.*—No notes or communication to any scientific journal having taken place by Dr. Jackson, who is wont to be most communicative on all occasions!

"administer the vapour of Ether to patients when about to undergo "the operation of extracting teeth. It was observed that no incon-"venience resulted from the administration of the vapour.

"CHARLES T. JACKSON."

The next communication to the Academy is—

"Boston, December 1st, 1846.

"The advantage of the application of the vapour of Ether has been "completely established in this country, and the agent has been used "with great success in the Massachusetts General Hospital.

"CHARLES T. JACKSON."

It will be observed that Morton is entirely ignored. Now the following document in full must be compared with the foregoing letters:

"State of Massachusetts,
"County of Suffolk.

"On the 27th day of October, A. D. 1846, personally appeared before "me Charles T. Jackson and William T. G. Morton, and made oath, "that they do verily believe themselves to be the original and first "inventors of the improvement hereinbefore described, that they do "not know or believe the same to have been known or used, and they "are citizens of the United States.

"R. H. EDDY,
"Justice of the Peace."

Doctors Jackson and Morton bought of Dr. Smilie the supposed right he might possess, from the fact of a publication by him in the *Boston Medical and Surgical Journal* of June, 1846, that opium and ether could be used to produce insensibility, so that it should not interfere with their patent.

Had Dr. Collyer taken out a patent in 1842, as he might have done, and made a trading speculation as Morton and Jackson attempted, he then, no doubt, would have caused the general adoption by the profession, of inducing the anæsthetic state in surgical operations. It was the same sordid, mercenary idea, exhibited by Wells in writing to Morton, which proved that the only idea was money making.

Mr. Morton never admitted the anæsthetic properties of nitrous oxide, at least he continually published *that he did not*, even as late as 1862, which seems quite inconsistent with all experience. In March, 1847, I published the fact unhesitatingly, that the nitrous oxide produces a state of *unconscious insensibility*. This is a most important fact, in connexion with the history of the anæsthetic discovery, as showing the limited knowledge possessed by Morton on these subjects.

When Morton was apprised of Dr. Jackson's communications to the French Academy of Science, all amity ceased between these conjoint discoverers: it was a war à l'outrance. All the secrets of the contending parties were exposed. Dr. Jackson had, however, gained a temporary celebrity, and one eminent French writer, in his enthusiasm, dedicates a Work, " To the Immortal Jackson."

There is truly but one move from the sublime to the ridiculous. Unfortunately for Dr. Jackson's future reputation as a discoverer, the same endeavour was made by him to deprive Professor Morse of the originality in regard to electro-telegraphy. It seems that, in crossing the Atlantic, Professor Morse and Dr. Jackson were fellow-passengers. Amongst other conversations, that of electro-magnetism became the topic; many years subsequently, when Professor Morse had worked out his idea in relation to electric telegraphy, Dr. Jackson claimed to have suggested to Morse all he knew on the matter!

Dr. Jackson, in his *Manual of Etherization*, says: " Nitrous oxide, " having *no anæsthetic properties*, fully sustains the conclusions of " Davy, that the gas will not prevent the sensation of pain."

Sir Humphry Davy said the very reverse. "As nitrous oxide " amongst its other properties has that of destroying physical pain, " it may be employed with advantage in surgical operations." It is inconceivable to imagine the cause, or desire on the part of Dr. Jackson to misinterpret, so violently, the language of Sir H. Davy. I repeat it, most emphatically, that if there is credit due to any one in this connexion, it is alone to William T. G. Morton; he, with a boldness which deserves every consideration on the part of the profession, launched the structure, though built by others, on the successful ocean of public favour. He must be forgiven for the questionable means he employed, though not admitted as legitimate in a professional point of view. I feel convinced that, had he not resorted to *these extraordinary and exceptional measures*, the *anæsthetic* discovery might have remained for years unheeded. All honour therefore to his memory! He repeated successfully, in 1846, the author's experiments of 1839, 1841, 1842, 1843, 1844. It was the Patent business which made the discovery an admitted fact.

It is important, at this stage of the inquiry, to see if in the whole course of their lives, either Jackson, Morton, or Wells ever made any discovery, or devoted their minds in that direction. Not a single record is to be found of any original thought being manifested by them.

CONTENDING CLAIMS.

Now, if we impartially review the history of Dr. Collyer's career—it has been one of continuous discovery, as regards original inventive talent—the inference is conclusive.

In 1842, he improves the mode of making sugar; 1851, invents a new method of crushing quartz; 1852, invents a new amalgamating apparatus; 1854, improved breech loading cannon; 1859, new composition for coating the bottom of iron ships; 1860, *paper material;* 1861, *paper material;* 1862, machine for cleaning wheat and other grain; 1862, "chemical ink pencil;" 1862, covering for electric telegraph cables; 1863, new tubing for chemical purposes; 1870, machinery for treating flax.

Most of these inventions are now generally adopted. All sorts of medals have been awarded,—gold, silver, bronze. All these inventions, and many more, have been *recorded* in the Patent Office.

Besides these inventions, Dr. Collyer made the extraordinary discoveries of induced mental hallucination or electro-biology, phrenomagnetism, and *vital photography,* &c. &c.—*Scientific Reporter.*

CHAPTER IV.

ANÆSTHESIA IN EUROPE.

IN the early part of 1847, Dr. Lach of Paris, published a Work, which for elaborate research and profound physiological deduction has not been surpassed, entitled *De l'Ether Sulphurique, de son Action Physiologique et son Application à la Chirurgie.* At page 13, he uses these words :—

" En 1843, M. Robert H. Collyer publia à Boston un ouvrage, où, à
" page 26, il declara, qu'un état de congestion, ou un état tel qu'on perd
" la conscience, peut être produit par l'inhalation de vapeurs narcotiques
" ou stimulantes. Il avait experimenté sur environ vingt personnes,
" mais les résultats définitifs furent peu favorables à ces inhalations."

What right had Dr. Lach to arrive at this conclusion ? To the mind of the author they were definite results, and were published as such, without any reserve or qualification, "that the inhalation of narcotic " and stimulating vapours produced a nervous congestive state—that " is, a state of unconsciousness and insensibility."

The constant use of the words "the same state of brain," " the identical condition," when referring to a person rendered unconscious, by inhalation or by other means, it is now useless to repeat.

Chloroform, having been discovered in 1830 by Professor Soubeiran, was studied later by Liebig and Dumas; its composition being 1 part carbon, 1 part hydrogen, 3 parts chlorine; it is also called terchloride of formyl. In March, 1847, Flourens, guided by inductive reasoning that chloroform resembled ether, made experiments on the lower animals, and demonstrated its anæsthetic properties, which he announced to the Academy of Science.

MM. Serres, Gruby, Longet, and Flourens made researches as to the action of sulphuric ether on animals, and Sir James Simpson was the first, on the 9th of January, 1847, to narcotize a patient with ether, so that the operation of turning might be accomplished without pain, which was the first application of the anæsthetic process to midwifery.

It was also Sir James Simpson who, at the suggestion of Mr. Waldie, of Liverpool, first inhaled chloroform on November 4th, 1847, in company with Drs. Keith and Duncan, of Edinburgh.

This marked a new era in anæsthetics, so much so, that, as a rule, the use of chloroform has, for over twenty-three years, monopolized the field to the exclusion of all other agents.

The memory of Sir James Simpson will always be associated with one of the boldest experiments in the noble cause of benefiting his fellow-beings in the hour of suffering—his name is indelibly inscribed as one of the greatest benefactors of the age.

Chloroform has played the most important rôle in anæsthesia, and though others will be substituted less dangerous and equally effective, it does not detract one iota from the great merit due to the discoverer that it possessed such powerful anæsthetic properties. Perhaps at least twenty millions have received comfort and consolation in the prolongation of life and health—which is the great aim of human existence—by the aid of the anæsthetic properties of chloroform.

The physiological effects of chloroform are as different as is the temperament and other constitutional peculiarities of the individual who inhales. One of the principal objections is, the tendency to negative the ganglions of the cardiac plexus, which give nervous force to the heart.

The anæsthetic agents are divided into those which at the ordinary temperature are gaseous, and those which are fluid.

The first comprise protoxide of nitrogen ($N+O$), methylic ether (C^2+H^6+O), chloride of methylene ($C+H^3+Cl$). The second or fluid are sulphuric ether $2\ C^4+H^5+OS^2+O^6$, alcohol ($C^4+H^6+O^2+HO$), ethylic ether ($C^4+H^{10}+O$), bichloride of methylene ($C^2+H^2+Cl^2$), terchloride of formyl or chloroform (C^2+H+Cl^3), amylene ($C^{10}+H^{10}$), turpentine ($C^{20}+H^{16}$), bisulphide of carbon ($C+S^2$), hydrochloric ether (C^4+H^6+Cl).

There are many more which possess anæsthetic properties. The substance chloral (C^2+H+Cl^3+O) acts on the nervous system as a powerful sedative. It is administered by the stomach. The anæsthetic effect is of long duration. It seems that the action is immediate on the brain, through the eighth pair of nerves.

Unquestionably other anæsthetics will in course of time be discovered, which are not attended with the risks on some nervous systems which follow the use of chloroform, bichloride of methylene, and other similar compounds.

Amongst the new anæsthetics is the bichloride of methylene, which has been introduced by Dr. Benjamin W. Richardson, "a fluid,

NUMEROUS ANÆSTHETICS.

"whose action is more gentle, but as effective as chloroform; it pro-
"duces less struggling and less vascular excitement, its narcotic effects
"are equally prolonged, it acts uniformly on the nervous centres, it pro-
"duces sometimes vomiting. When it is carried so far as to kill, it
"destroys by equally *paralysing the heart and the respiration.*"

This disposition to paralyse the heart, is the great objection to chloroform; as some persons are peculiarly susceptible to be thus acted on. The bichloride of methylene* has specific gravity of 1·34, whereas chloroform is 1·49; it contains one atom less of chlorine and one atom more of hydrogen. Of the carbon compounds, this is perhaps the safest. Flourens says, " the hydro-carbons which take away pain, also take away life.". These when inhaled deaden the vital powers, they extinguish, in their advance from the superior portions of the brain, step by step, the principle of existence, until they arrive at the anterior portion of the medulla oblongata, where exists a point from which arise nerves, which, if paralysed, also compromise life itself.

It is, therefore, of major importance that no anæsthetic should be employed endangering the life of the patient.

The catalogue of anæsthetic agents may now number over thirty, and the most eminent physiologists describe their action to be nearly identical. In fine, there are many comatose states of the nervous system, which present phenomena, so closely allied in their various phases, and seeming to run into each other, that it is most difficult to define limits. Catalepsy, hysterical coma, the syncope which accompanies neurosis, are all governed by the particular temperament and physical condition of the patient. Hysterical coma, or trance, is a special condition of the brain and nervous system—there is sometimes consciousness, with entire loss of sensibility and power of motion. All co-ordination has apparently ceased. It is more than probable that consciousness which persons suppose they possess, during a trance, may arise from the confused dreamy ideas consequent on returning consciousness. A few moments in a reverie may appear to occupy days or months.

There are two marked and opposite conditions of the nervous system, both accompanied by loss of consciousness, both anæsthetic states. The first arises from an excess of nervous fluid arising from increased action of the lungs, producing true "nervous congestion," as when Nitrous Oxide, Alcoholic Vapours, Ether, Chloroform,

---

* The bichloride of methylene differs, chemically, but slightly from chloroform; in fine, it consists principally of this substance.

Bichloride of Methylene have been inhaled, and in magnetic or nervous coma. In these there is a diminished arterial supply to the brain, or an anæmic state. An interesting case is recorded in the *American Journal of Medical Science,* October, 1860, page 400, in which the condition of the circulation in the brain was observed during anæsthesia—a person who had extensive fracture of the cranium, which permitted a view of the encephalon. It was seen that, as chloroform was administered, during the effect of the narcotizing influence the brain was remarkably pale, and whenever the anæsthetic effect began to subside, the surface of the brain became florid and injected.

That the anæsthetic state is one of nervous congestion arising from excess of nervous fluid I have never doubted, for it is this nervous congestion which deprives the surface of its sensibility, by the supply being cut off. The nervous tissues of the lungs are specially acted on during the inhalation of anæsthetics. The first stage is one of mental excitement. The second, of delirium, which rapidly runs into that of loss of consciousness, or the third stage. If carried beyond this, life may be compromised.

Whenever the functions of the lungs are so low, or there is an impaired condition of creating nerve fluid, then we find the medulla and ganglionic nerves only supplied. A condition of existence resembling the lowest orders of animal life.

On one occasion I was so fortunate as to witness in New York, in October, 1853, a most remarkable case, exemplifying under abnormal conditions how low the human physical existence can be brought.

Cornelius Vroman, aged 37, was exhibited by a Dr. Came as having remained in a state of somnolence for upwards of five years. A more emaciated skeleton-like being I never witnessed. Life was a mere organic existence, he simply vegetated. The intellectual faculties were at zero: the circulation and nerve power as low as the turtle. It was with great difficulty that any pulsation could be discovered; the temperature was 60° Fahrenheit. From what I could gather from Dr. Came, Cornelius had brought the condition on himself by excessive onanism. The respiratory murmur was discoverable by the aid of careful auscultation. I placed Cornelius in every imaginable attitude, which he would retain for hours; the muscles were in a semi-rigid condition. On one occasion he was put on his legs, Dr. Came not placing him upright, he fell over, his head coming in contact with a marble table, causing a contusion two inches in length; this blow had not the least effect in bringing him to consciousness. Every three months his state of sleep was interrupted by a short waking of about twenty minutes, during which period he devoured everything eatable placed within his reach; he would then relapse into another three months' doze, from which no effort could rouse him. He was daily supplied with a few teaspoonfuls of liquid food, which he swallowed with great difficulty.

The whole details of this marvellous case are fully recorded in the New York *Scalpel* of October, 1853.

The contrast with the following case will be sufficient reason for its introduction.

The cause which induced this sleeplessness would, if reversed, have produced the opposite condition of brain.

SLEEPLESSNESS.

To the Editor of the Boston Medical and Surgical Journal.

Sir,—As you desire for publication an account of my extraordinary sleeplessness, I make you welcome to what follows :—

"During three periods I have been bereft of sleep :—first, in 1833, "for six weeks; again in 1837, for five months; and now, these last four "years and five months.

"Prior to the first period I never suffered from want of sleep; "although at times little sufficed for refreshment. My constitution, "naturally sound and vigorous, was till forty years of age sustained by "healthy exercise as a farmer—riding and walking much; indeed walks "of thirty or forty miles a day in no way distressed me. In the year "1819 I was cruelly imprisoned in Canada ('*illegally, unconstitutionally,* "*and without excuse or palliation,*' as the present Legislative Assembly "has declared), during eight months; the last of which, in solitude "and stifling heat, undid me; and for three years thereafter I was "debilitated; nor should I ever have regained energy but for a resolu- "tion to go to hard labour, which I did for upwards of three months— "breaking stones for the roads in Wiltshire, England, and living on the "earnings—sixpence a day—viz., from Sept. 9th till Dec. 23rd, 1822, "as minutely detailed in Parliamentary Journals.

"In the year 1824 I was again confined in London, three years and "eight months — the purpose being to make me appear to the world "insane; and thus have my influence with the people destroyed. I "weathered this persecution by living on vegetable food; and being free "from all excitement, the time passed away happily. During this con- "finement I had need of very little sleep; and the greater part of my "time in bed, never more than six hours, was given to reveries, chiefly as

" to schemes for bettering the condition of the labouring poor, plans for
" laying out land in the wilderness, and studies for city building, which
" I contemplated, and still do, to reduce to a science.

" It was during this period, I think, that a habit of living without
" sleep began to form. From March, 1828, till November, 1833, I was
" tortured in Scotland with unsettled affairs; but generally in the best
" health, and could walk from morn to night without fatigue, while four
" or five hours of sleep was quite enough for rest and enjoyment.

" Nov. 5th, 1833, I left Edinburgh at six o'clock P.M. in a canal
" boat on my way for America—choosing such conveyance that I might
" be along with my trunks, containing valuable books and papers. The
" boat was an iron one, and jarring every little while against some other
" boat, bridge, or lock, subjected me, reclining in a vile hold, to unspeak-
" able discomfort. Sleep was out of the question, and I had none all
" the way to Glasgow, which we reached about ten o'clock next morning.
" Taking time on shore only for breakfast, I forthwith had my trunks
" conveyed to a steamer in the Clyde, and immediately sailed for
" Greenock. There getting on board the steamship *Vulcan*, we were
" under weigh for Liverpool in half an hour. We ran to sea in the teeth
" of a hurricane, sheltered during night in Lamlash bay, and by earliest
" dawn, ran through a stormy ocean to Liverpool, which we reached
" early the second day. These two nights, like the former, were
" sleepless.

" Engaging a passage to New York in the packet ship *Pacific*
" to sail next morning, I told Captain Wait how I had been deprived
" of rest. He recommended a warm bath before going to bed in
" Liverpool. This procured I believe some sleep, but certainly from
" Liverpool to New York, embarking November 9th, and landing
" December 22nd, I had not a wink of sleep. It was dark when we landed.
" I resorted to a warm bath, got into a comfortable bed, and slept, as I
" had done before leaving Edinburgh; nor did I again want sleep
" nightly for three years.

" Crossing the Atlantic, my sleeplessness became subject of conver-
" sation. One prescribed laudanum, but that had no effect; another
" opium, which also failed; a third said, if I got tipsy, that would do;
" but that did not. I drank grog, which only made me sick, and that,
" for the first time, at sea.

" The beginning of January, 1837, while lodged in a tavern at Wil-
" loughby, Ohio, I was seized with erysipelas in the leg, a disease I
" have been long subject to, and during five months was without
" sleep. After that period sleep returned gradually. For many weeks

"I dozed by times, and had strange dreams; one of them so distinct
"and beautiful that I wrote it down, and it was really worthy of
"record. The attack of erysipelas, conjoined with other diseases,
"rendered me lame and extremely feeble during the remainder of my
"stay in Ohio—eighteen months; and after that, for four years and
"four months, in Canada, with frequent attacks of erysipelas and rheu-
"matism, I was never strong, and all the time lame; often indeed at
"death's door, in the most wretched condition, separated from my
"family, and, for the most part, without sympathy or a friend to
"whom I could unbosom my griefs. The loss of a beloved daughter
"crowned my calamities, and finally barred out '*Nature's soft nurse*.'
"My children, four daughters and a son, the youngest now twenty-
"seven years of age, grew up every way well; and my great conso-
"lation was, that whatever befel me, still my family would be pros-
"perous and happy. Alas! when least expecting a reverse in that
"quarter, even when glorying over pleasant letters recently received
"from my daughters, I heard that the second was dangerously ill. I
"lay in agony two weeks, and then had the melancholy assurance of
"her death.

'Tired nature's sweet restorer, *balmy sleep*,
He, like the world, his ready visit pays,
Where fortune smiles. The wretched he forsakes;
Swift on his downy pinion, flies from woe,
And lights on lids unsullied with a tear.'

"After seven months of this period of sleeplessness, I consulted Dr.
"Widmer, of Toronto, reputed the most experienced physician in
"Upper Canada. He advised to dine early, and eat nothing after,
"before going to bed; which till this day has afforded the most com-
"fort. His medicine—acetate of morphia, which I took at two distinct
"times, for ten days together—had no effect. Corresponding with
"the doctor, he expressed an opinion that my sleeplessness proceeded
"from excitement of the brain, caused by much reading and writing
"on politics, which I told him was an entire mistake, as I read and
"wrote little, and troubled myself not at all with politics. In fact, my
"troubles sprung from unsettled private affairs, as my family and
"friends well know.

"After three years of this sleeplessness, being in Montreal, I advised
"with Dr. Robinson, but he could do nothing for me. Telling him
"that few would credit my accounts of sleeplessness, he said he could,
"having a patient, Mr. Jamieson, who had not slept the last five
"months.

SLEEPLESSNESS.

"For a year past, I have been attacked with no disease; and within these last six months, spent on the seaboard, have been gradually regaining strength—partly, I think, from salt air; nor do I despair of sleeping, were all circumstances favourable. Long weakened with attacks of erysipelas, I am not able to take that degree of exercise which, in former days, contributed so much to brace my system; neither have I now sufficient stimulus, in any way. With these, I feel confident that sleep might be recovered.

"Wherever I abide this sleeplessness has been matter of jest; and few sympathize in my calamity, one of the most trying our nature can be exposed to. Fortunately, a native buoyancy of spirit sustains me against every jest, and the world's humours are repelled by my own.

"Since coming to this city of '*notions*,' where everything is talked about, but nothing decided, I have been beset with inquiries, doubts and denials. Some proposed watching me night and day, so that I might be *caught napping*, and this they were welcomed to do; but did not. I then cast abroad a handbill, offering a *benefit* to any charitable society who might choose to bring together a multitude for wonderment, and thus have a fair trial instituted; but none have come forward; and *doctors*, as they have hitherto *differed*, may differ in opinion still.

"Various books on the subject have been laid before me—McNish on the 'Philosophy of Sleep,' and John Mason Good, M.D., on the 'Study of Medicine.' The first author, in my humble opinion, is anything but *philosophical*. He amuses with many stories, but comes to no conclusion on the principal subject discussed. He mixes up *absence of mind*, or what should rather be called *intensity of thought*, with sleep, which to me appear distinct things. He speaks of sleeplessness being a 'habit' and 'habitual;' states that General Pichegru did with only one hour's sleep a day through a whole year's campaign, and mentions others who 'remained weeks, months, or even years, *if authors are to be believed*, awake.' Now why should he refer us to authors, thus to question their authority, after he had settled the point *dictatorially* in a previous chapter, where he says, 'sleep *cannot in any case be entirely dispensed with*;' and elsewhere deciding against the entire want of it as '*fabulous*.' Who *assured* him of this?

"Dr. Good is not thus contradictory. He sets forth views and theories supporting them with instances of sleeplessness. Mr. Cooch, he says, gives a singular case of a man who never slept, and yet enjoyed a

SLEEPLESSNESS.   37

"very good state of health till his death, which happened in the
" seventy-third year of his age. He had a kind of dozing, for about a
" quarter of an hour, once a day; but even that was not sound sleep,
" though it was all he was ever known to take.

"Now, sir, in all this we have yet no *certainty;* and opinion after
" opinion may be advanced without any good whatever. I say a final
" issue may be reached if I, here in Boston, were subjected to trial;
" and for the sake of science—to have a fact established curious in the
" history, habits, and constitution of man—I am willing to subject
" myself to the test.

"On various occasions I have been *almost* asleep, but do not think
" I have absolutely been so during these last four years and five months.
" In September, 1840, I travelled, with only one short pause, from St.
" Catharine's, Upper Canada, to New York, in stages, steamboats, and
" rail-cars; talking much and continually excited with varied scenes
" and occurrences. Arrived at New York, I immediately lay down in
" a luxurious bed, closed round with mosquito curtains; and next
" morning declared to a fellow-traveller, that I would be unwilling to
" *swear* that I had not slept. Nine months afterwards, seated in the
" door of my log-house in the woods of Canada, during the stillness of
" a summer evening, and when the air all around was loaded with
" smoke, I verily believe I would have slept, had not a neighbour roused
" me. Five months later, in Kingston, thinking all my vexations in
" that quarter ended, and that I should soon rejoin my family in
" Scotland, I had a delightful night, and told my landlady that I had
" *nearly* been asleep; and reaching Quebec a week afterwards, enjoying
" the same hope and worn out with travel, I dozed and dreamt, which
" is certainly an approach to sleep. Six months ago, reaching Provi-
" dence from New York, surrounded with agreeable objects, and enter-
" tained for a whole day in the most delightful manner, I flung myself
" into bed; and if Morpheus did not obtain dominion over me, I had
" at least perfect repose.

" These approaches to sleep are acknowledged, not for the surrender
" of what I have maintained invariably: but to confirm the main
" position. In Ohio two persons came into my bedroom while my
" head was covered over, and because I did not speak to them said
" I was asleep. So here in Boston, while reclining on a sofa with
" closed eyes. On both these occasions I knew the train of my thoughts
" perfectly. In another place, the servant who put on my fire in the
" morning reported that on two occasions he had found me asleep. I
" was confident he had not, and tested the matter another morning

"unknown to him. I covered up my head, kept silent, let him question me, and then discovered that it was only from my being attentive that his voice was audible through the covering.

"Both the doctors above quoted, allow that sleep may be dispensed with for long periods; and if for weeks and months, why not for years and for ever? I have not only done without it for years, but for months have simultaneously suffered from acute pain and torture of mind still worse than that; nor could I have endured, but for a cherished principle—that to endure is duty.

"I have tried many remedies: a hop-pillow, hop-tea, &c. &c. &c. Winter before last, at Kingston, Canada, in great misery from the deprivation, I resorted to laudanum again and again—fifty drops, seventy drops, ninety drops, and upwards of a hundred; yet still I had no sleep. Here in Boston I have been advised to get mesmerized; and if professors of that art are willing to try, they may try. Most surely to succeed, I say, 'Let me rest from persecution because of principles and opinions, which has been unrelenting during thirty-five years; give me my rights as a British subject in Canada, and deeds to land there vexatiously withheld; restore to me property in Britain taken out of my possession under most iniquitous pretences; and let me rejoin my children in such a happy home as I once enjoyed.'

"All this is now submitted, frankly and sincerely, to your learned and liberal profession.

"ROB. F. GOURLAY.

"Marlboro' Hotel, Boston, May 10th, 1843."

SLEEPLESSNESS—*continued*.

To the Editor of the Boston Medical and Surgical Journal.

"SIR,—You have heard of my sleeping two hours, and wish for publication, a detail of circumstances, which I now furnish.

"June 16th, the British steamer being to sail, I was employed from daylight till noon writing and despatching letters. Ten minutes past twelve the last was mailed. I then ran to a newspaper-office, purchased the paper of that day, and mailed it also.

"By this time the President of the United States was approaching: and I stood, in heavy rain, till the procession had passed the Post-office. After that I was engaged with business till near two o'clock, sometimes in, sometimes out of doors, and got drenched. Returning home, I put off my wet clothes, and went to dinner at half-past two o'clock. About three, I retired to my bedroom: sat down to read, "having pulled off my coat and boots; but in a quarter of an hour was overpowered with drowsiness; flung myself into bed, under the coverlid; immediately became warm, perspired, and soon after slept soundly and certainly! Awakening, I deemed it, for a few minutes, morning; rejoiced that the weather looked propitious for the Bunker-hill celebration; but feeling my clothes became undeceived: started up; looked from my window to the Old South, and saw by the clock that it was half an hour past five P.M. In fact, I had been in the land of Nod, as near as may be, the time above-named.

"One of the newspapers, with the too customary practice of misrepresenting, reported that I had *been caught napping*—but this statement was immediately conveyed to my fellow-boarders, and is perfectly correct. Some inquired, if I felt refreshed; but no perceptible effect was produced, and the occurrence has in no way changed my long-established habit. I have not slept since; and now that the weather is hot, I have many restless and miserable nights.

'From short (as usual) and disturbed repose
I wake: how happy they who wake no more!'

"ROB. F. GOURLAY.

"Marlboro' Hotel, July 15th, 1843."

The author was well acquainted with Mr. Gourlay for some months, in the city of Boston, in the early part of 1843.

The two cases afford the most interesting contrast of the opposite state of the nerve-power or fluid being in the first case deficient to carry on the functions of life: whilst in the latter, the lungs, generating an excess, did not admit of ordinary sleep, itself a state of nervous congestion.

When Mr. Gourlay exposed himself to the action of humidity, he slept for two hours, caused by the abstraction of vital electricity; whilst the exposure of Cornelius Vroman to a damp atmosphere, in 1353, carried off too much electricity, and death ensued, as his abnormal state did not admit of any further diminution without compromising life.

On the inhalation of narcotic and stimulating vapours, the superior lobes of the brain are first affected; in the next place, the posterior and cer.-bellum; then the sensitive portion of the spinal cord; then the roots of the nerves of sensation; after the anterior portion of the spinal cord, the roots of the motor nerves; and lastly, the medulla oblongata, from which arise the nerves, the suspension of whose function involves the vital functions. In the first two stages no danger exists, but if carried beyond these, a few inhalations more may compromise the life of the patient.

Loss of sensibility does not necessarily imply loss of consciousness.

There are numerous theories relative to the physiological action of anæsthetics. Nunneley, Ozanam, and Scoutetten have been the most prominent advocates, that the carbonization of the blood was the cause of insensibility. Flourens, Longet, Lallemand, Perrin, Broca, Duroy, suppose that the loss of sensibility is produced by acting directly on the cerebro-spinal axis : whilst another class of eminent physiologists attribute the anæsthetic state to arise from the retardation of the oxygenation of the blood.

The author still adheres to the physiological explanation he advanced in 1841, 1842, 1843, and 1844—namely, that the brain is nervously congested, the stimulant action of the anæsthetic agent on the nervous tissue of the lungs causes the generation of a large and sudden excess of nervous fluid. *Vide* extract of lecture delivered in Providence, March, 1843.

Of course each case presents its special nervous phenomena. In some the spinal cord seems to be attacked without materially influencing the cerebral hemispheres, so far as the loss of consciousness is concerned; others seem to be acted on through the par vagum; whilst another class are apparently acted on through the circulation. Those anæsthetic agents which directly increase the respiratory function, are the least dangerous: as they merely increase or create an excess of vital fluid, which produces nervous congestion of the brain.

A powerful mental emotion will blanch the surface of the body, whereas a slight one will cause a rush of blood to the capillaries, and cause *a blush*. How much is conveyed in this every-day occurrence! It explains most perfectly the nervous command over the circulating system. All those anæsthetic agents which act specifically on the nerves of the heart should be avoided. I have never been an advocate of the chlorine compounds for this reason. In some the action is so immediate that they are struck down as if by lightning. Fortunately these cases are comparatively exceptional; still they have occurred, and exemplify a principle which runs through many phases; showing that we must seek for chemical combinations more harmonious to the vital economy, which have the property of producing anæsthesia.

Amongst these, none command attention more than the nitrous oxide, that is, one proportion of nitrogen combined with one proportion of oxygen. It is a near approach to the natural respiratory ele-

ANÆSTHETICS IN GENERAL.   41

ment, the excess of oxygen causing the excitement and subsequent unconsciousness. The nitrous oxide the last few years has been employed in hundreds of thousands of cases. I am not aware of a single fatal result arising from its inhalation.

On the 25th of July, 1865, Dr. Carrochan of New York removed the entire breast with the glands of the axilla, the patient being kept insensible for sixteen minutes. This distinguished surgeon also performed several amputations of the leg under the influence of the nitrous oxide. The inhalation of this gas is unaccompanied by nausea, sickness, or vomiting, or any of the unpleasant symptoms which so often accompany and follow the inhalation of chloroform.

The nitrous oxide gas will become the favourite anæsthetic. The writer, who has had perhaps as much experience as any one in the administration of all kinds of anæsthetics, would not hesitate one instant the inhaling of nitrous oxide to produce unconsciousness; he certainly would not breathe any other vapour to produce insensibility.

It is no use combating with gentlemen who start with a favourite theory. Dr. Ozanam says, " Tout la série des corps carbones volatils " ou gazeux est douée du pouvoir anésthetique ; plus ces corps sont " carbones plus ils possèdent ce pouvoir."

The carbon compounds, it is true, have a *mixed* effect; they do most certainly interfere with the oxygenation of the blood. Though the blood after death in animals, by being kept in the nitrous oxide, presents a dark colour, its condition is very different from that of death from chloroform and the carbon compounds, as when exposed to the atmosphere it becomes florid, and there is no disintegration of the globules.

On the same principle, pure carbonic acid destroys life by paralysing the heart's action, by dark blood coming into contact with the left ventricle. (*Vide* experiments by Flourens and Ozanam.) There are certain conditions essential to stimulate the organs of the animal economy. Though light is the natural stimulus of the optic nerves, too much has been known to produce blindness.

Dr. Ozanam also says, " If animal magnetism was a regular science " accessible to every one, without doubt it furnishes to the surgical " profession the most complete realization of an anæsthetic state. We " can put a person to sleep and leave him in that state for hours or " even days without his suffering and without danger to him. All the " functions of life are carried on as in the normal state, nothing is " interfered with but the loss of sensibility."

Dr. Ozanam, you have expressed a great truth with an independence worthy of your distinguished position as a philosopher. It was the conviction of this truth which caused the author to investigate the subject during the years 1839 to 1844. (*Vide* Report of Boston Committee, Appendix.)

The question must be independently put: What is the state of unconsciousness induced by animal magnetism, or by whatever name it may be called? The time is past to deny that such a condition exists. It is, just as Dr. Ozanam says, the uncertainty of the application which renders it of comparatively little value practically as an anæsthetic.

It was in the year 1842 that the author nearly sacrificed the life of his brother when submitting him to experiments with Indian hemp and alcoholic vapours. Had a fatal result followed, no one, even now, will say that the author would not have been submitted to a criminal trial for murder.

Had the following cases occurred amongst the first who inhaled chloroform, what would have been the result?

In the instance of Miss Stokes, the operator says, *She was struck down as if by a flash of lightning*. So it was with Walter Badger, Charles Desnoyers, Jean Morgan, Caroline Bates, and hundreds of other cases. Most of these were in the prime of life, with no other ailment than a decayed tooth. Dr. Sansom gives cases where from fifteen to thirty drops of chloroform have produced immediate death, whilst in others $10\frac{1}{2}$ drachms have been inhaled, then suddenly a deep narcotism was induced, followed by death.

In a case of tetanus at Guy's Hospital more than a pint of chloroform was administered in twenty-four hours.

So long as the nervous system is not paralysed there is no danger. Once prostrate it to a negative state, and the chances are indeed small. A single drop of hydrocyanic acid taken by a near relative caused her to fall dead, as if she had been crushed by the force of the most powerful steam hammer. The whole of the nervous system was negatived at once. The nerve molecules were changed instantaneously, and could not recover their normal state.

This allotropic condition is familiar to chemical science; a single particle of sulphur will change entirely the nature of caoutchouc, an infinitesimal particle of arsenic will alter the character of gold. In fine, every metallurgist knows how small a particle of a foreign body will alter entirely the nature of the metal. Apply these principles to the vital economy, and we explain many apparent mysteries.

Dr. Scoutetten, physician to the Military Hospital of Metz, relates

IDIOSYNCRASY.

the following :—" I found myself seated close to a young lady in a
" theatre to witness a curious performance called 'Etherization.'
" The actor, to better carry out the delusion, threw a small quantity of
" ether in the parquet, which vapour on raising the curtain dispersed
" into the body of the theatre. At the instant and without any warn-
" ing, the young lady fell asleep, all sensibility was extinguished, all
" feeling and consciousness disappeared; this greatly impressed me.
" Sometime afterwards I questioned the lady, and learnt that it only
" sufficed to open a bottle containing ether in a room or a church for
" sleep to be produced the moment the vapour reached her."

In making my experiments in 1842 and 1843 with the fumes of poppy heads, olibanum, myrrh, coriander seeds, alcohol and sulphuric ether, though no appreciable vapour escaped into the apartment or lecture room, it often happened that persons were narcotized and thrown into an insensible coma. Call this what you may, idiosyncrasy, vital susceptibility, or temperament, it is an admitted fact that the nervous system of some persons is so sensitive that it only requires the most minute foreign agent to produce an allotropic state of the nervous system.

Hydrocyanic acid is ranked amongst the anæsthetics; in fine, all those agents which destroy sensibility, and are non-supporters of combustion, are also destroyers of life. It is not so with protoxide of nitrogen gas, which supports combustion and stimulates the functions of the lungs in excess of their normal functions, producing nervous congestion without loading the circulation with a foreign substance, as is the case when chloroform is inhaled. The chlorine and carbon compounds depress or render negative the nervous system, they produce the anæsthetic condition at the expense of the vital element.

Until the occult forces which govern the functions of life are better understood, the most eminent members of the medical profession will remain at variance as to the safest anæsthetics.

Dr. Sansom justly says :—" Consider how our faculties and func-
" tions are maintained during life and health. The circulation
" throughout our body of the blood, which receives from the air we
" breathe a due supply of oxygen, is a necessity of perfect life. In a
" normal state the blood charged with it permeates everywhere through-
" out the system, undergoing that wonderful process of combustion,
" ending in the excretion of carbonic acid, which causes the heat of the
" body ; it reacts on every tissue, developing *electric* and other correlated
" forces obedient to and yet producing the unknown *vital principle*.

"Perfect venous blood, with perfect arterial blood, produces electrical phenomena evident and demonstrable."

Had Dr. Sansom gone a step farther he might have added: Is it not the functional speciality of the lungs to assimilate this electricity to the purposes of the great nervous centres? Are not these the reservoirs of this vital electricity? *Vide* letter, January, 1844.

" *The lungs at every respiration send vital electricity to the brain, which has been thus assimilated to subserve the purposes of life.*"

That there is a close connexion between the functions of nervous matter, in the use of an electrical or magnetic fluid, cannot be disputed.

In the *Comptes Rendus*, Jan. 2nd, 1838, M. Becquerel made the following communication to the French Academy:—

"Dr. Prevost, of Geneva, has succeeded in magnetizing very delicate "soft iron needles, by placing them near to the nerves and perpen-"dicular to the direction which he supposed the electric current took. "The magnetizing took place at the moment when on irritating the "spinal marrow a muscular contraction was effected in the animal."

The vital electricity generated by the torpedo, the gymnotus, and silurus electricus, who have special nervous organs for the *secretion* of this electricity, has been closely investigated.

According to the experiments made by Mr. Faraday, the gymnotus exhibits the electrical properties of producing chemical decomposition, making a magnet by induction, evolution of heat, electric spark. The shock of a single gymnotus was equal to a coated surface of 3500 square inches!

When it is considered that the secretion of vital electricity is effected in water—one of the best conductors—it does not require a very great stretch of the imagination in seeing how the chemical act of respiration is also attended with the secretion of vital electricity.

Humboldt says the gymnotus abounds in the small rivers which flow into the Orinoco. It employs its voltaic powers at the direction *of the will*, as other animals do their horns, teeth, or fangs to secure its prey or repel aggression. Hence horses and mules are attacked by them when forced to enter the streams. The quadrupeds suffer severely from the shocks they receive: the gymnotus becomes so exhausted as to be easily caught.

The fact of animals secreting electricity, which is subsequently used at the direction of their will, is a fact of great importance in connexion with the anæsthetic state induced by *nervous congestion*. What is the function of the brain? How are its desires conveyed to the various parts of the body?

NATURAL SLEEP.

The direction of will is the result of the education consequent on experience. When the infant first attempts to walk the whole attention or direction of will power is demanded; so much is this the case, that if the attention is distracted from the act of walking the limbs lose all power of supporting the body. After a short time the child walks and talks without apparent exercise of will in the act of walking. In fine, the communication of nerve power or fluid is established between the brain and the muscles to be moved. It is the use of this nerve force, through the agency of the will, which governs all our actions.

Exhaust the brain by over-exercise of the muscles, or by fatigue, the brain requiring to be replenished with force or vital fluid; nervous congestion or ordinary sleep is induced, because the senses cannot any longer be supplied.

If the brain did not discharge at the direction of the will the nerve fluid, how could the muscles be moved?

There are two kinds of nervous congestion, as already stated, one from an excess, the other from a diminution of the natural supply. Natural sleep is an intermediate state; it is now that the functions of the lungs are especially called into requisition, in order to renew the supply to the brain of electricity vitalized, so as to subserve the purposes of volition, and rendering the body sentient to outward impressions. Or are there different fluids, one of motion, and another of sensation, and another adapted for organic life? It is more probable that the same fluid, by passing into special channels, is either motor, sensitive, or ganglionic. Or is there a special vibratory state? An imperfect supply is accompanied by a corresponding derangement of the function of the organ.

The natural sleep of the infant or of a person who has not exhausted the brain by fatigue, is marked by a gentle respiratory murmur, whereas the respiratory action of the man who has laboured all day, is much more active; the respiratory murmur is deep and sonorous.

The nervous matter of the brain has a variety of very distinct offices to perform. The senses have each their locality and nerves, which communicate with their outward organs. The olfactory nerves have a special portion of the brain, which takes cognizance of the various kinds of odour; the same with the eye and the ear. One of these may be destroyed without necessarily affecting the other. The power to recognise sounds may be wanting, still the organs of sight and smell remain perfect.

As we ascend to higher functions, these are found to be developed

HYBERNATION.

in different persons, so that one may be comparatively idiotic in one faculty, and in another possessed of remarkable mental capacities. What animal surpasses the eagle in visual powers? Does not the hearing of the antelope or the smelling of herbivorous animals surpass those senses which in man are comparatively feeble?

Each animal has a development of nervous matter in accordance with the habits and peculiarities of its existence. No one can confound the broad heads of the carnivora with the long, narrow heads of the graminivorous; so it is with their brains. To give the brain matter of the giraffe to the tiger would be an absurdity. The powerful jaws and claws of a tiger require a corresponding brain function. In fine, cerebral physiology demands a special study. No one who has devoted the least attention to the subject but must admit that the brain is a congeries of organs, each adapted to a distinct office.

In hybernating animals, during the state of torpor the lungs act sluggishly, supplying merely sufficient nervous force to sustain life. This torpid condition during the depth of winter is so great that the animal experiences no sensibility. This is particularly the case with various species of snakes in America. From the *Yankee Nation*, May, 1842.—" Dr. Collyer dwelt particularly on those animals which in the " dead of winter remain in a torpid state; some of these could be cut to " pieces without showing any signs of life, although their brains " contained the vital element."

Daily Ledger, April 18th, 1842.—" It is by means of the vital force " in the brain and the rest of the nervous system that hybernating " animals are enabled to pass the winter in an insensible state, or to " remain embedded in a tree or a stone for centuries without losing " vitality.

" Fish are sometimes frozen so hard that they are broken like a " piece of glass; yet these identical fish, if gradually thawed in water " at from 35° to 40° Fahrenheit, swim about as if they had never been " in an unnatural condition.

In travelling from Hamilton, Canada, on a moonlight night, to the falls of Niagara, in sleigh, in the winter of 1842 and 1843, my companion, who was wrapped in buffalo robes, fell into a deep comatose state from breathing the cold atmosphere. He was rendered so insensible, that it required over an hour's friction before a large fire before consciousness was restored.

Captain Franklin, in describing the winter he passed in the Polar regions, says, " The fish froze as they were taken from the nets, and " became a solid mass of ice, and by the blow of a hatchet were split

EFFECTS OF COLD.

"open, when the intestines were removed in a lump. If in this frozen state they were thawed before a fire, they recovered animation. He saw carp recover so far as to leap about with vigour, after having been frozen for thirty-six hours."

Dr. B. W. Richardson says, "The benumbing influence of extreme cold may be accepted as a natural discovery coeval with the existence of mankind in the temperate and frigid zones. Physicians at an early date seem to have used cold for the relief of pain. Its systematic use probably came in later, after the revival of letters, so-called. It is related of Harvey, the discoverer of the circulation of the blood, that he was accustomed to seek relief from the pain of gout by going on the leads of his house and there immersing his painful foot in ice-cold water. But we have to name another man living in the same age, to see the same remedy employed in a direct manner, in order to remove sensation in a part of the living body before subjecting it to a surgical operation. This was Thomas Bartholinus, one of the most learned and industrious masters in physic. Bartholinus wrote a treatise of 232 pages on the medical use of snow (*De Nivis usu Medico*). This book, from beginning to end, is wonderfully suggestive, and in the 22nd chapter he advocates the practice of *applying extreme cold* to produce insensibility before the performance of surgical operations." The plan, he says, was taught him by Marcus Aurelius Severinus, of Naples. In our day the same application of cold has been brought into use by a man of singular originality and genius, Dr. James Arnott.

Dr. Richardson exhibited to the author in 1868 the freezing of the brain of a pigeon by the use of the ether spray; the insensibility was immediate, and the brain frozen in less than a minute. When, however, this same bird was first operated on, it took eight minutes to bring about a state of unconsciousness.

One of the most remarkable circumstances connected with the employment of anæsthetic agents, is the facility with which unconsciousness is produced after subjugation has been once or twice accomplished. The vital powers at first resist powerfully the action of a new state produced by foreign agents. This natural law is essential to the preservation and well-being of the individual. The principle of accommodation as exemplified in the pigeon also applies to man.

The nervous influence from a second person is hardly perceptible on the first, second, or third trial, except with remarkably susceptible persons, who under favourable circumstances are reduced to a state of *nervous congestion*, or unconsciousness, in a few minutes.

CHAPTER V.

ANIMAL MAGNETISM, MESMERISM, OR NERVOUS CONGESTION, AND OTHER ALLIED TOPICS.

WHEN the writer was first reduced to a state of semi-unconsciousness by Dr. Cleaveland, in October, 1839, he probably was as sceptical as most medical students on matters which do not come within the curriculum of their University studies. When asked to be *magnetized*, the reply was:—" I have no objection to be submitted to the trial." On which certain conditions on the part of the subject or recipient were stated, as being necessary to be observed, in order to produce the effect—

1. An absolutely quiet, or passive state. All influences tending to disturb or divert attention should be avoided.

2. The person to be operated on should be placed in a comfortable sitting position, in a subdued light.

3. The exercise of the will of the operator should be directed to the brain of the person operated on. Persons of robust constitution do not often yield to the nervous influence on the first trial; sometimes eight or even twelve efforts will bring about the *nervous congestive state*.

The writer was particularly informed, that if he resisted the influence, it would destroy the result; as, in that case, it was a mere antagonism of the nervous fluid of the two brains. The recipient must be in every sense negative, whilst the operator is positive. These conditions being no more than reasonable; as no results, no matter how simple, can take place except the necessary conditions are complied with.

The operator seated himself immediately in front of the recipient, took hold of both hands, and steadily gazed with great fixedness in the eyes of the recipient or person acted on. In the course of four or five minutes the extremities, that is, the hands and feet, felt cold and numb; then followed (in ten minutes) a drowsiness and disposition to sleep; in the course of thirty minutes from the commencement of the operation, the writer was unable to move, but consciousness still remained. He feels convinced that had not his attention been aroused by the whispering of some persons present, that the unconscious state would have been produced.

No further trial was made. Enough, however, had been effected to produce a powerful impression that there was truth in the subject. The best work, Deleuze, "On Animal Magnetism," was bought and read attentively.

Two weeks subsequent to this occurrence, a case quite unexpectedly presented itself. Narrating the fact of having been partially magnetized at an evening party, a lady said, "Can you magnetize me?" The writer, not even supposing that he possessed magnetic power, replied that he did not know, but would make an attempt. Accordingly the trial was made, and in less than five minutes the voluntary muscles were all paralysed, and the most profound coma supervened.

The first impression on the writer's mind was that the lady was feigning, in order that she might have a laugh at his expense. This impression was soon dismissed, from the extraordinary phenomena which followed. The entire absence of sensibility was demonstrated by passing a needle under the finger-nail. On opening the eye, the globe was found entirely under the control of the oblique or involuntary muscle, causing it to roll upwards and inwards.

The experiments which followed, showing the sensations of the operator, were also conveyed to the brain of the recipient. On taking a glass of wine, tasting salt, vinegar, pepper, or tobacco, they were at the instant recognised and described. But the most unlooked-for result followed on touching her head.

To use the words of Dr. Elliotson, in his address before the Phrenological Association of London, July 3rd, 1843:—

"Dr. Collyer first discovered (and quite accidentally), in November, "1839, at Pittsfield, in North America, the possibility of exciting dis-
"tinct cerebral organs by contact with the corresponding portions of
"the surface of the head.* The evidence of this date appears suffi-
"cient. At a party, when mesmerism was the topic of conversation,
"he threw into the mesmeric sleep a young lady who had always
"refused to allow him to examine her cerebral development. He took
"this opportunity of examining it with his hands, and to his astonish-
"ment, as he touched over the organs of Self-Esteem, Combativeness,
"Wit, &c., the respective faculties went into action. He was, how-
"ever, already so excited with the occurrence of clairvoyance, at this

---

* "Psychography." Philadelphia, 1843.

"period, that he confesses he paid very little attention to the circum-
"stance. In Louisiana, the following spring, he produced the same
"results."

In all my experience for over thirty years no case has surpassed this, *my first*. A more sensitive or refined person one rarely meets in life. The parents would not listen to a repetition of the experiment. No bad effects followed.

My next recipient was a negro boy of fourteen years. No difficulty whatever was experienced in reducing him to a state of unconsciousness. I also acted on the cerebral organs, which, with some successful experiments in tasting and smelling, was all that could be got out of this subject. It was nearly a year before another opportunity offered to *mesmerize* under favourable circumstances. Even then, beyond producing a state of unconsciousness, no phenomena were elicited.

In the early part of 1841 I met a medical gentleman in New York who had reduced to a state of the most profound unconsciousness an Irish boy, uneducated, of about fifteen years. When magnetized he was so stiff and insensible that had he been frozen his whole body would not have been more rigid. This boy offered a fine opportunity of investigating all the phenomena. It is true his speech was scarcely audible, but with a little practice he was understood. This case presented many peculiarities. The sympathies *were perfect*. No matter what the writer tasted or smelt, he would recognise it at once; or if he received an impression, such as having his nostril tickled or his hair pulled, the recipient would not only manifest the dislike, but also mutter "*Don't pull my hair*," or "Don't tickle my nose." On one occasion it was discovered that "Frederick" saw everything that was passing in the room, though his eyes were firmly closed; and the occurrence to which he referred took place, so to speak, behind his head. His clairvoyant powers were, however, of very short duration; during the whole time he was with me, over eighteen months, they never lasted more than from three to five minutes, after which his answers partook of a kind of haphazard guesswork, sometimes partially true. This is important, as many who do not understand the fact of how evanescent is the period which is really accompanied by lucidity, attribute the failure to incapacity or summarily denounce the subject. On some occasions, for the short period the power was exercised, he saw the time (altered purposely) in a hunting-watch. And on another he told the contents of an envelope correctly, which consisted of four different coloured wafers placed *in a card;* recesses having been made in the card to receive the wafers, so that the contents of the envelope could not be known to the operator. The exercise of *the will* of the operator was something surprising. Under favourable circumstances, no matter how complicated, the movement of the arm or fingers of the operator, it would be exactly repeated in the recipient.

It is a question as to whether the recipient actually saw the wafers, or did he obtain the information by reading the brain of Mr. Neal, who prepared the envelope? Of this no proof of a positive character has ever been presented. Supposing the sight did occur, it was evident that the external organs of vision were not exercised, but the brain itself. We know in dreaming that the pictures received through the senses are reproduced in all their apparent vividness of reality, showing that the brain is the seat, the true sensorium, of all the senses; is it not possible, during exalted states of the organ, for its functions to exhibit abnormal phenomena?

During the "nervous congestive" state of brain (mesmeric), also during somnambulism, and the intervals of hysterical coma, there are manifested functional phenomena of the brain which startle the timid and ignorant. No doubt a knowledge of these phenomena, artificially induced, has been a fruitful source of superstition in the early dawning of civilization.

The experiments with "Frederick" became so popular that private investigations were instituted, composed of the most scientific men in America. These eventuated in the publication of the Boston Committee Report, a document which for rigorous impartiality and independent honesty has never been surpassed. *Vide* Appendix.

The thirty gentlemen who composed this committee were with one exception entire sceptics before entering on the investigation.

The phenomena of the *nervous congested* brain caused the author to examine the records of past ages, so as to discover if possible the secret *of the mysteries.*

It was when repeating the feats of the Egyptian magicians that the whole subject of "*inhaling narcotic and stimulating vapours, to produce unconscious insensibility,*" was especially investigated.

These experiments consisted in the inhalation of the fumes of coriander seeds, poppy heads, olibanum, the vapour of alcohol and ether. The insensibility and unconsciousness produced on some occasions was so profound as to create alarm, and was treated by a certain class of the press with derision, as the "bowl of molasses' experiments."

It must be here mentioned that the unconscious or anæsthetic state, whether produced by inhalation of narcotic and stimulating vapour or by the nervous fluid from a second person, was applied to the performance of surgical operations of every description—amputations of the thigh, removal of a cancerous breast, extirpation of the fungus eye of the child. In 1842 these surgical operations were performed in every portion of the United States; hardly a newspaper appeared but contained the account of an important surgical operation during the anæsthetic state, induced by the so-called mesmeric influence.

It was in April, 1843, at Philadelphia, that a tooth was extracted from Miss Allen. Dr. Robert Hare, Professor of Chemistry, University of Pennsylvania, assisted at this operation: the fumes of alcohol, poppy heads, were the principal agents employed. It was in the following month, May, 1843, that these words were written by the author in "Psychography."* The inhalation of narcotic and stimulating vapour produces an anæsthetic state *identical* with that produced by the nervous influence.

The necessity, however, of obtaining an anæsthetic, in view of rendering surgical operations painless, was not recognised by the public or the medical profession at this date; still the author made use of every state of *insensibility*, no matter how produced, as the following shows:—

The *Liverpool Standard*, October 17th, 1843, says:—

"To prove that mental hallucination could be induced by the "operator, he took a young woman, only *semi-mesmerized* (waking "state), and placed a jug in her hands, which she recognised to be a "*pig*. By a pass of his hand she began to stroke it as a pet cat, which "she declared was such; and the influence being removed, her own "surprise at her mistake was pictured by a look and expression of "shame before the large audience which could not be feigned. Again "her mind was influenced, and she saw a large fish at her side, from "which she endeavoured to escape, with every gesture of horror, until "the influence was removed. A young man and young woman, *both* "*perfect strangers* to Dr. Collyer, were placed in a rigid or cataleptic "condition of the muscles (though otherwise perfectly awake). Dr. "Collyer stated that he knew of TWO OPERATIONS having been performed "in America during this state—viz., EXTIRPATION OF CANCER FROM THE "FOOT, AND ADJUSTMENT OF A COMPOUND FRACTURE OF THE FORE-ARM. "In the latter case a portion of bone was removed in order to set the

---

* A copy of which, *with the manuscript of this work*, has been in the possession of Dr. Benjamin W. Richardson for over six months, with certificate of copyright entered in Philadelphia, June, 1843.

'limb (generally a painful operation), and yet the patient *was in-sensible.*"

The state of Induced Mental Hallucination or Electro-biology was discovered by the author on the 4th of January, 1843.

"Canandaigua, New York, Jan. 5th, 1843.

"I do solemnly declare that Dr. Collyer can act on any part of my "body. Though I am aware of his intention, I cannot resist the "power of his will. He can cause me to feel hot or cold, wet or dry, "tall or short, stout or spare; in fact, he can change my condition at "any time.

"JOHN PARSHALL."

In May, 1843, the following was published, relative to the same subject:—

"Mental hallucination can at any time be produced on persons in "the *waking state*, who are recipient to the agency, with much more "power and marked results than during the mesmeric state. I have "made persons, *when perfectly awake*, believe themselves to be par-"taking of a good dinner: they would in their minds be filling their "plates from empty dishes. I could successively change the nature "of their food, make potatoes turn into apple dumplings, a turkey "into a leg of mutton, water into brandy, sugar into a stick of candy. "I in one instance took four persons and pressed their thumbs, they "immediately commenced feeling as if intoxicated; I then restored "them in an instant; could obliterate from their memory the occurrence "which had just transpired, and alternately bring them vividly to their "recollection, and cause them to scream with agony on placing a piece "of money in their hands, they feeling all the torture of burning metal "when placed on the skin. I made two persons at the same time be-"lieve themselves to be bottles of ginger-beer; they distinctly heard "the fermentation within, and desired me with all earnestness not to "draw the cork, for that would kill them. I made a man fancy him-"self a general officer, a locomotive, &c. In fact, I know not a single "condition but what may be brought about by the action of the mind "of the operator.

"The same state of mind may be made the medium of curing the "most distressing mental diseases."

The *Liverpool Mail* of October 14th, 1843, in reporting another of my lectures, says:—

" . . . . The experiments were of a most interesting description, and

"varied from those of last evening, being of a higher order. The
" lecturer, after requesting the subject to ascend the platform, placed a
" glass of water in the hands of the female and desired her to drink.
" In answer to a question she said the draught was very good—it was
" wine. Dr. Collyer subsequently placed a powder on her tongue,
" which she declared to be extremely sweet and pleasant; the remainder
" of the substance was shown to the audience, when it turned out to be
" Cayenne pepper; a similar effect was produced on a young man who, on
" having some aloes put into his mouth, declared it to be barley-sugar.
" An extraordinary illusion was next produced, when being requested to
" look down at his leg, which was in a rigid state, he seriously asserted
" that he could not see it, so completely was the patient under the con-
" trol of the will of the magnetizer. The doctor then took his hands,
" placed them together, and desired him to separate them, but notwith-
" standing the most strenuous exertions, they remained unseparable
" until the influence was removed."

This lecture was reported in detail. I make the above extracts to show that no one prior to this date had made these demonstrations. It is a remarkable fact that any portion of the body may be rendered locally *anæsthetic* by a mere action of *the will* of a second person. Yet *such is a fact*, which no amount of incredulity can repudiate; for it will be seen that, to use the words reported in the *Liverpool Standard* of October 17th, 1843, "two operations had been performed in "America during this state — viz., *extirpation of cancer from the* "*foot, and adjustment of a compound fracture of the fore-arm*. In the "latter case a portion of bone was removed in order to set the limb "(generally a painful operation), and yet the patient was *insensible*."

This is repeated as being of major importance in showing how the anæsthetic state was made available by the author in order to assuage the sufferings incidental to *surgical operations*. It is also of inestimable value, taking into account *its date*, being fifteen months prior to Mr. Wells's inhalation of the protoxide of nitrogen, as showing that no competitive interest prompted its publication; also that there was no partiality as to the mesmeric (so-called) process over other means of inducing the anæsthetic state. This *great fact* has been entirely overlooked by the writer of the History of Anæsthetics in the *Lancet* of June 11th, 1870. The author of this pamphlet has never disputed the unquestionable priority of the illustrious chemist Sir Humphry Davy in the use of nitrous oxide to alleviate pain, though Sir Humphry never produced unconsciousness.

The writer in the *Lancet*, after a certain fashion, has given the

ALCOHOLISM.

author (Dr. Collyer) the credit of having initiated modern anæsthesia in the United States of America. No doubt, had *not authentic* official documents warranted this, he would never have compromised himself to the statement of facts which were susceptible of being challenged to direct proof. It will be seen with what independence and fearlessness these pages are penned. Nothing is asked *as a favour*, but the *most impartial truth* demanded.

In the *Liverpool Standard* of October 14th, 1843 :—

"That the *anæsthetic state*, during which *surgical operations* could "be performed, could be brought about or produced: 1st, by natural "*fatigue;** 2nd, the transmission of the nervous force from a second "person; 3rd, by concentration of the mind on one subject accompanied "by muscular action; 4th, by steadily gazing on an object (hypnotism); "5th, by the *inhalation of narcotic and stimulating vapours.*" To these might have been added induced mental hallucination and hybernation. All these things must be taken into account by the reader, as it proves conclusively that no prejudice existed in the mind of the author as to any special mode of producing the anæsthetic state.

There is another anæsthetic state, that induced by alcoholism. One case presented itself in New York in the spring of 1841, of a sailor who, having returned from a long voyage, abandoned himself to the indulgence of drinking whisky in large quantities. The consequence was an entire prostration of the nervous system. To the great majority of the medical profession he was *a corpse*. No perceptible respiration, no pulse, surface cold and clammy; in fine, when first seen by the author he was pronounced as having been dead some minutes. The first course indicated was a *hot bath*, and constant friction of the whole body, which was continued for over three hours, when the first indications of returning consciousness were observed by the trembling of the eyelid. Some moments after, by the aid of the stethoscope, the heart's action became perceptible, and subsequently the respiratory organs resumed their functions.

No doubt in great prostration of the nervous system, heat, electricity, and the vital force of a second person are essential elements in the recovery, or restoration to the normal condition.

The *Soporific Cakes* (*celebrat et panis oblationem*) used by the early Egyptians had also a powerful anæsthetic effect. The candidate for initiation was enabled to endure the terrible ordeal, which

---

* *i.e.*, fatigue causing a loss of consciousness.

he would not have been able to endure but for the medicated cakes, which produced a state of *mental hallucination or inebriation*, rendering him easily subjugated to the will of the priests and magicians who conducted the ceremony of the mysteries. It was this *mental state*, caused by eating the *panis frugibus*, which caused those who were being initiated to reveal their most secret thoughts.

The use of alcohol, in all its forms, as a beverage, has been beyond doubt one of the greatest curses and drawbacks to the advancement of civilization with which intellectual man has had to contend.

CHAPTER VI.

EGYPTIAN MYSTERIES.

"He that believeth not is damned," was the constantly reiterated admonition to those who were passing through the ceremony of initiation, in the Temple, by the Priests of Egypt.

The ceremony was commenced by eating the *panis oblationem*, so that the candidate could be easily subjugated to the will of the operators who conducted the ceremony of the mysteries. It was on these occasions that empirical knowledge was resorted to with so much effect. Most of the phenomena of the brain were unquestionably known in those ages, which, from the absence of scientific principles, were ascribed to supernatural sources.

All the phenomena of the nervous system, no matter how *apparently* ethereal or *spiritual*, are materially connected with elements which govern the animal economy; and, if not now, will at no distant period be perfectly understood and susceptible of a physiological explanation. From the earliest days of our existence we are merely the reflex of those with whom accident has thrown us in contact. Do not the impressions of the nursery haunt us through life—and they too often become our masters in the weak and unguarded moments incidental to misfortune, disease, decrepitude, or at approaching dissolution?

Man has always been the creature of those by whom he was first instructed. If his parents or guardians were Japanese, Hindoos, Turks, Africans, French, English, or American, he certainly was not consulted on these points: nor had he a choice as to his educational prejudices thereby induced.

It is alone in the advancement of scientific truth that true progress is to be sought. Science may be compared to the young Hercules struggling with the monster typhons—Ignorance and Superstition. When the child shall have attained maturity, these demons will have been exterminated. Ages may yet pass before the consummation of that state; then men will have ceased to butcher each other for some abstract idea, the merits of which are not even understood by the combatants, but merely to gratify the selfish vanity of some ambitious potentate. The time will arrive when men will not be thus sacrificed; but before that can take place, education must have made great strides.

Science, in its onward march, exposes the tricks, the frauds, devices, and artful mummeries of the priests, the magicians, and soothsayers of Babylon, Chaldæa, China, Syria, and Egypt, whose craft has so impressed the whole habitable world at this moment. Did not the leaders of the Israelites receive all their instruction from the Egyptians? Certainly the writings attributed to Moses were inspired by his education during his forty years in Egypt, from the period of his mysterious finding by Pharaoh's daughter, to the time he left the temple as one of the *initiated* in magic and medicine.

What is the condition of the brain at birth? Is it a "tabula rasa," or is the nervous matter predisposed to hereditary conditions as inherent consequences of parentage, which develope themselves in defiance of any system of education?

No one can imagine that there are *innate ideas* under all circumstances; in the higher animal scale, the conditions for the manifestation of the faculty or function of a specific organ must exist. It is true that in certain cases we discover a physical attraction or repulsion before the animal has had time to receive education: as much an affinity, which cannot be resisted, as is exhibited when inorganic bodies are brought together under favourable circumstances.

The brain of man becomes modified in the exercise of the faculties by systematic education. The senses are the inlets or channels of all the knowledge the brain has obtained.

The senses hold direct communication physically with the laws and conditions of all matter; the eye is an optical instrument, and the ear an acoustic, in accordance with the laws of light and sound. It follows that as these organs receive and convey impressions according to physical laws, that the sensorium, the brain matter, must also have a condition or organization adapted to receive these impressions, and also to retain them.

Are not the images received by the eye painted on the retina, which is an expansion of the optic nerve? This simple fact requires no argument to prove its necessity; in fine, the images received produce on the sensorium their corresponding impressions, and there is a definite form of vibration of the nervous particles or molecules that compose the cerebral matter. If there were to be a suspension of cerebral vibration, there would also be a corresponding suspension of the

INSTINCT.

thinking and voluntary power. No one who has observed the vital functions of the lower orders of life, perfect from their earliest moment of existence, but must have been convinced that the *sensitive condition* bears no comparison to that which exists in man; moments in these may be equal to years. The example of the sight of the eagle in relation to that possessed by man is sufficiently great; but nothing to the extreme *sensitiveness* with which their functions of life are called in requisition. These have been, for want of a better name, called "instincts," which is nothing more than the attractive or repulsive states peculiar to the special creation.

One of the most illustrative cases is that of the hatching of duck's eggs by the fowl. The moment the young birds emerge from the shell they make for the water; the foster-mother cannot follow. Here is an attraction and a repulsion. It is evident then that had there not existed an inherent attraction for the water, the ducks would not have entered it; and if there had not been a repulsion, the fowl would have gone to the rescue at the supposed danger of her adopted brood. This same affinity is manifested in a thousand different phases in animal life.

The nervous ganglions are extremely sensitive: in many insects so great, that their defined functions are brought into play coeval with their coming into existence. The laws of life must be studied from the physical stand-point; the physiologist is the vital chemist, whose office it is to analyse these varied phenomena. The vital element exists as much as the atmosphere we breathe. The earth itself had to pass through a state of existence which developed this very element, the vestiges of which are now found as the constituent composition of the upper strata, which covers our globe for hundreds of feet. Even at this period of the earth's existence, do we not find that the very conditions of the zones at specific periods are essential to certain forms of animal existence?

There was a period in the early transformations of the earth which rendered it no more difficult to conceive the creation of the largest forms of life (as the mammoth), than now would be the production of animalculæ. The same causes invariably produce the like effects.

CHAPTER VII.

SOMNAMBULISM.

During the dreaming condition of the brain the *senses are asleep.* Is it not evident that the extravagance or coherence of the dream depends on the number or combination of organs which are in an active state? For no matter how inconsistent or incoherent the dream, it produces the impression of a reality until the other portions are brought into activity, which correct the false impression produced during the dream. Persons congenitally blind never dream of visions, nor those who from birth never possessed the sense of hearing dream of sounds. Are not these facts of major value to the cerebral physiologist?

The brain cannot produce, under any circumstances, phenomena incompatible with the sources of supply. On the other hand, does not the brain receive multitudinous impressions of which it is not cognizant, and which are only recognised when the organ is in an abnormal state? Does not the dreaming state of the brain form its own exclusive source of connective associations, a kind of double consciousness? We revert in our dreams to the scenes of former dreams, and these continue throughout a long life, which have no actual basis beyond the singularly false impressions produced.

During brain fever the patient loses all sleep for weeks, and frequently there is accompanying mental hallucination. The action of the brain is then so powerful as to overcome the ordinary function of the senses, and throws its false impression beyond their natural visual function. It is not the external eye that is deceived, but the brain's action which overpowers it. The patient often mentally sees persons walking in the room, converses with them, and this hallucination is well-known to medical men. It is evident that the brain has, in this state, rendered the senses subservient to its super-excited state, therefore the spectral illusion.

Abercrombie gives the case of a servant girl who, during cerebral fever, repeated whole passages of Homer in the original Greek. It was found that she had been in the service some years previously of a clergyman who was in the habit of reading Homer aloud. Here is in this case food for philosophical research to satisfy the most abstract inquirer. In the state of somnambulism, the brain is oftentimes so sensitively excited that phenomena are exhibited which only astound and perplex those who are content and will not examine beyond mere normal manifestations.

Abercrombie, "On the Intellectual Powers," page 294, gives the case of a girl, seven years of age, who, during a state of somnambulism, would with her lips imitate the violin and the piano. In a year after the attack, she would discourse with the utmost fluency and correctness on a variety of abstruse topics, both political and religious ; the history of the world. In these discussions she showed the most wonderful discrimination, often combined with refined sarcasm and astonishing powers of mimicry. Her language was fluent and correct, and her illustrations often forcible and eloquent. She was fond of illustrating her subjects by a fable, and in these her imagery was both appropriate and elegant. She was by no means limited in her range. Napoleon, Wellington, Blucher, and all the kings of the earth figured among the phantasmagoria of her brain; and all were commented upon with a perfect freedom from restraint, that often made one think poor "Nancy" had been transported into Madame de Genlis's palace of truth. The justice and truth of her remarks on all subjects excited the utmost astonishment in those who were acquainted with her limited means of acquiring information. She has been known to conjugate correctly Latin verbs, which she had probably heard in the school-room of the family ; "and she was once heard to speak
" several sentences very correctly in French, at the same time stating
" that she had heard them from a foreign gentleman whom she had
" met accidentally in a shop. Being questioned when awake, she
" remembered having seen a gentleman, but could not repeat a word he
" said. During her paroxysms, it was almost impossible to awake her,
" and when her eyelids were raised and a candle brought near to the
" eye, the pupil seemed insensible to the light. For several years she
" was, during the paroxysms, entirely unconscious of the presence of
" other persons; but at the age of sixteen she began to observe those
" who were in the apartment. She could tell correctly their numbers,
" though the utmost care was taken to have the room darkened. She
" now also became capable of answering questions that were put to
" her, and of noticing remarks made in her presence ; and with regard
" to both she showed astonishing acuteness. Her observations, indeed,
" were often of such a nature, and corresponded so accurately with
" characters and events, that by the country people she was believed to
"be endowed with SUPERNATURAL POWERS.

"During the whole period of this remarkable affection, which seems to have continued for ten or eleven years, she was, when awake, a "*dull, awkward girl, very slow in receiving any kind of instruction,* "though much care was bestowed upon her, and in point of intellect "was much inferior to the other servants of the family. In particular "she showed no kind of turn for music. She did not appear to have any "recollection of what had occurred in her sleep."

Had she remembered, she would not have been a *dull, awkward girl.*

Here we have a most perfect example of the high sensibility of vitalized electricity. During the abnormal state the brain was supplied with a *superabundance* of nervous fluid.

This case exemplifies the extraordinary *sensibility* of those *nervous ganglions*, as seen in ants, bees, wasps, spiders, &c., where the most apparently complicated functions of life are called into activity nearly coeval with their birth. According to the *standard* of man's *comparatively* sluggish brain function during normal states, no idea can be conceived of a brain becoming educated in a moment of time. Yet such is the case. If the *conditions exist*, we exercise faculties of brain which appear marvellous.

Unconscious impressions are continually being made on the cerebral mass, even in its lourd unimpressionable state.

In the highest states of *vital electricity*, as exhibited in the ant, bee, &c., does not the whole functional capacity of the ganglionic organ come into use, merely by the fact of its being brought into contact with the appropriate conditions favourable to the exercise of the functions?

Is it not as much an affinity as the combination of bodies? Are not the inorganic chemical laws and the organic vital laws governed by principles having a common origin?

No one can have observed the various forms of crystallization of metals and their salts, of water in freezing, of the various forms of plants, and the structure of animals, without being impressed with the fact of the similarity.

As various chemical compounds always assume the same crystallized form, so do certain plants; also in animals there is no difficulty in tracing the causes of the fixed laws of their being. It is no more difficult to explain the bee forming hexagonal cells, or the bird always building a particular form of nest, than it is to explain why certain metals and their salts take fixed forms of crystallization. It would not be philosophical to deny to a higher organization that property, which we admit takes place in a lower.

The double consciousness of "Nancy" is exemplified in every-day

SOMNAMBULISM. 63

experience. We return daily in our dreams to imaginary regions, peopled with special beings; indulge in Elysiums, or endure all the horrors of Tartarus.

Those acquainted with somnambulism induced by the nervous fluid of a second person will not be surprised at the apparently marvellous cerebral powers manifested during that condition of *nervous congestion*. In somnambulism thus artificially induced, the most remarkable mental faculties are exhibited, yet these persons during the natural state of brain, are uneducated and entirely ignorant of the subject, in which they have shown such proficiency during the nervous congestive state. Most of these have the power of self-inducing this state of brain, or *voluntary somnambulism*. The Indian Brahmins and Fakirs even teach the mode of inducing this state. In Avicenna's treatise "De Animalibus," a case is reported of a man who had the power of paralysing the limbs at pleasure by an effort of volition. Cardanus relates of himself that he could voluntarily place himself in a state of ecstatic insensibility. St. Austin, in his work "De Civitate Dei," has recorded the case of a priest, Restitutus, who could whenever he chose throw himself into a state of complete insensibility, and be like a dead man.

Emmanuel Swedenborg and Jacob Behmen had this same power of *volition*. The case of Colonel Townsend, who could (*to all external appearances*) die whenever he chose, and after having lain for a considerable period in that state, could resuscitate himself by a voluntary struggle. "He could die," says Dr. Cheyne, "when he pleased." In fine, the power of the brain over the rest of the body is not surprising, seeing that it is the great centre of existence; from it all the functions of life proceed. The power of *self-inducing* a state of brain analogous to that of the girl "Nancy" mentioned by Abercrombie, will furnish the means of explaining most of the phenomena which the "mediums" have so successfully employed.

Disturbing causes will defeat the manifestation of the phenomena; so they will with the highly sensitive mesmeric somnambulist. As no one will contend that vitality is not the most active and sensitive state of matter, therefore it is necessary not to disturb the cerebral condition in order to elicit phenomena; nothing is more easy than to defeat the manifestations by an antagonistic exercise of the brain.

The most apparently trivial circumstances disturb the condition of the somnambulist; so much so, that all lucidity and power cease nearly simultaneously with its existence. All the noted mediums, together with those famous jugglers "the Davenport brothers," have been oftentimes investigated by the writer, but on no occasion have any phenomena been presented which are not explicable on physiological principles, especially those known as ecstatic states of brain.

Some of these "necromantic mediums" have played a bold rôle; their pretended intercourse with *departed souls* has found abundant credence in modern times, as it did with the early Egyptians.

The case of "Nancy," who during her state of somnambulism showed such extraordinary powers, and when awake in her natural state *was a dull, awkward girl,* affords a ready explanation of the powers of brain *self-induced* by the power of will which some persons possess.

This double consciousness of brain exemplifies that we are the recipients of impressions the most abstruse and complicated in *the natural waking state,* and which only require a special condition of brain for their manifestation. There is no memory of one state when in the other. Here is food for thought and mighty speculation, if we chose to ignore practical physiology for the dreamy mysteries of metaphysical dogmas.

We can bring to mind a gentleman who is wonderfully brilliant intellectually for some twenty to thirty minutes, after which time he becomes confused, foggy, and incoherent. In every-day life we find special times in which the brain acts with great power; nor can we command these functions. They have been called, for want of a better name, "inspirations;" in fine, the functional powers of the brain are continually subject to every variety of disturbance, in accordance with the physical condition of the brain itself; the mere influence of our surroundings, the vital atmosphere of those with whom we come in contact, will influence our mental powers to a degree which it is difficult to imagine without having been experienced. Whilst in Bruges, Lower Flanders, the intellectual powers are nearly *nil.* Whether this arises from the *low* situation of the town or of a corresponding mental condition of its inhabitants, it is difficult to understand. One would imagine that it was the latter, as on removal to Ghent or Brussels, none of those oppressive mental influences existed.

Intellectual and moral associations in childhood stamp the character of the brain's functions all through life.*

---

* If men could be born without mothers, then the policy of not elevating woman to exercise a higher position, socially and politically, would have some weight. It has been the slavery of woman's position which has reacted on man, producing the most debasing consequences. Let woman but feel her responsibility, by cultivating her self-esteem and self-reliance in the higher walks of life, and the

The somnambulism of Jane Ryder, seventeen years of age, so ably reported by Dr. Belden, is probably the most remarkable case on record, where during the *ordinary condition of the waking state* no particular aptitude or prominent faculty of brain was manifested. Yet during the abnormal state her mental powers were exalted to such a degree as to astonish every one. She conversed on most subjects fluently and correctly: during the paroxysms she inwardly thought it was daytime. At the commencement of the paroxysm she appeared like a person going quietly to sleep. *Her eyes were closed*, THE RESPIRATION became *long and deep;* her attitude and the motion of the head resembled a person in a profound sleep. She differed exceedingly in different paroxysms. She recollected during one paroxysm what occurred in a former, though there was no recollection in the waking state of what had occurred during her somnambulism. At the termination of the paroxysm, she sank into a profound sleep, accompanied by *long and deep respirations.* Like all somnambulists, she appeared fatigued; her morbid symptoms were manifestly aggravated by the constant trial of her powers.

---

inevitable consequence—*self-respect*—will become the leading characteristic of the sex.

If women are "physically and mentally weaker than men," it is the evident duty of man to cultivate to the highest degree *the source* from which he owes all that he possesses *physically and mentally.* The higher the condition of the mother, the more fitted is she to imprint *those early impressions*, which are the basis of the man's character, intellectual powers, all through life. The principal retardation of civilization, is this remnant of past savage times, when woman was treated as a vassal and considered as unfit to hold any other office than that of the mere *animal mother.*

My fellow student, Dr. Thomas Laycock, seems to think that woman should not exercise *virile occupations.* Perhaps Dr. Laycock will *define* what he means by such a sweeping expression. Let him remember what was considered *a virile occupation* for woman when he was a student of medicine; *now* she is most efficient in its execution.

What Dr. Laycock means by *moral and maternal instincts* it is impossible for me to divine. "A great change has come o'er *the spirit* of his dreams" since last we met.

Women are no more possessed of *instincts* than men. I would discard all these antiquated ideas. Let woman be encouraged in the efforts that the few energetic and courageous are making to tread the path of intellectual progress. Those who make impediments by such spurious arguments as that *a prurient imagination* may be incited, place a very low standard before the student of medicine. The student who could allow his studies to be *impeded by the presence* of ladies, would not be the most sanctimonious young gentleman when *outside* the university, or the most eligible, morally, *in the practic of his profession.*

During the paroxysm she would learn with *a rapidity* truly surprising any subject, no matter how difficult or abstruse. She acquired a perfect knowledge of chess, so as to beat the best players; though in the waking state she did not even know the moves. The paroxysms would sometimes last for twelve hours, though generally seven or eight hours. Jane could read in the darkest room with the eyes bandaged.

This case, like that of "Nancy," previously given, indicates that the brain was not *sufficiently* supplied in the ordinary waking state with vitalized magnetism or nervous fluid, in order to manifest more than faculties common to most dull, uneducated girls.

A few moments during the dreaming and somnambulic states of brain, will cover a period of time which in the natural state would require months to accomplish. It often occurs that during the most incredibly short period a whole life's history has been passed in review before the mental faculties. In fine, the capacity of brain function is so marvellously increased when there is any extra supply of vital electricity or nervous fluid, that we cannot, according to ordinary standards, measure the lapse of time. How could we conceive the waves of light striking the retina, taking the velocity of light at 186,000 miles in a second, and reckoning 33,866 wave breadths to the inch for the extreme red, 43,197 for the yellow, and 70,555 for the violet? We find for the impulses on the retina per second which produce these sensations of colour, the following numbers:—Extreme red, 399,101,000,000,000; soda yellow, 509,069,000,000,000; extreme violet, 831,479,000,000,000. Yet these are distinct intervals of time, as compared to which a minute is an eternity.

The extreme delicacy and intense sensitiveness of the nervous apparatus of the visual organs of man and animals in the normal state is thus exemplified; still this is as nothing to the increased functions of the brain during abnormal states, when the functional supply of nervous fluid is much increased. There are also states of brain when the most abstruse and complicated mental formulæ are presented; these are received and retained unconsciously, and years may elapse before a condition of brain occurs in order to throw off these impressions.

We knew intimately that extraordinary writer Edgar Allan Poe. He was obliged "*to tune himself up*," to use his own expression, before he could write a line. His brain would not *throw off* until it was stimulated to the functional condition. We have known Poe drink a pint of whisky. All his famous productions were written under the stimulus *of drink*.

The same is often related of that brilliant poet, Lord Byron.

These cases no doubt will suggest dozens similar in character to the reader; where men were conscious of their incapacity, except when "tuned up" to the occasion.

Had not an inflammatory condition of brain occurred in the servant girl given by Abercrombie, she could not have repeated whole passages of Homer in the original Greek.

It is the same with the so-called "spiritual mediums" the writer has met with; these people in their ordinary normal condition are really most uninteresting and singularly ignorant on all scientific matters.

It is only when the brain is super-charged with the nervo-vital element, or in the nervous congested state that its functions are exalted to such an extent as to astonish and confound the *uninitiated*. The recipient of magnetism who has been frequently reduced to a state of unconsciousness, soon becomes possessed of the power of self-inducing a somnambulic condition of brain. It is this faculty which enables the "mediums" to produce phenomena which, during the normal state, they have no capacity of producing; nor does it require that the condition should be one of unconsciousness. Most of the most noted "mediums" who have been examined by the author there has been a semi-magnetic or state of abstraction.

Whenever these "mediums" exhibit wonderful mental faculties, it is from the power of self-inducing this condition of brain. This power of will over the functions of the organs, which are normally under the control of the organic system of nerves, was exhibited in the case of Colonel Townsend of Bristol, who could suspend the heart's action so that those who witnessed the phenomenon supposed him to be dead. It is also exercised by the Fakirs of India, and no doubt it was this power of self-inducing a somnambulic state of brain which Swedenborg employed. When persons have had their brain frequently subjugated, they soon possess *this power*.

The subject is so large, that it is impossible to enter more fully into details on the present occasion; this must be reserved for a work in preparation on the "Functions of the Brain in Health and Disease."

If the brain is not adequately supplied with vitalized magnetism, it is incapable of the lowest order of mental manifestation. In functional derangement of the lungs, as in the case of Cornelius Vromann, the supply was so weak or so limited, as not even to admit of the waking state. This state of sleep must not be confounded with the natural, or that induced by an extraordinary supply of nervous fluid. When

VITAL CRYSTALLIZATION.

there is a morbid activity of the lungs, as in the case of Mr. Gourlay there is an excess of vital fluid, and sleeplessness is the result. A violent mental shock caused by intense joy or grief will cause sleeplessness. In these cases we invariably have increased respiratory action.

A proper supply of nervous fluid from the lungs is essential to mental exercise. If the brain is too small, there is a want of power; or if too large for the capacity of the lungs, there is also deficient supply to produce cerebral function. There must be a co-ordination of the various organs in their development, otherwise mental functions are imperfect.

During the dreaming state known as *nightmare* what horrid tortures and excruciating suffering is endured, and the disturbing cause may be of a trifling character.

The exquisite sensitiveness of the iodized silver plate to the action of light, is as nothing when compared to the functions of *vitalized electricity*.

The great function of memory cannot be exercised except the vibratory condition of the brain substance is perfectly unimpaired, and free from obstacles which abnormal states produce. The least *pressure* will destroy all coherence, and suspend the function as completely as in the most profound coma. One case occurred, which the author examined with great care. The patient had lost a portion of the cranium. On pressure of the finger all power of *thought* was suspended. A conversation might be arrested at any instant. The subject or topic would, however, be continued by the patient on the moment of the pressure being removed.

There is a spiritual materiality, or, in other words, a vitalized magnetism, so extremely ethereal or attenuated that its operation in combination with ganglionic nervous masses present functions of so unusual a nature that the unlearned in such manifestations have attributed them to agencies beyond the sphere of nature's laws, and they are denominated "supernatural."

No one is prepared to say, that the hexagonal construction of the bee's cell, where the honey is deposited, or the radiating lines of the spider's web, are not as much vital crystallization, so to speak, as the special formations of inorganic bodies into definite angles, when passing from the liquid to the solid state. Why should not the same law be the remote cause in both instances of organic as well as inanimate existence? To deny to a higher condition of matter the laws of assuming definite forms which are known to exist in the lower, seems most unphilosophical.

NECROMANCY. 69

The ancients, who were ignorant of the laws which govern matter, ascribed all things beyond their limited comprehension, to the supernatural.

Necromancy was the art of calling up the spirits of the dead, most commonly practised by the Egyptians. The magicians were the interpreters of the occult language employed at these ceremonies— the "Manes." The questions made by the living were distinct and easily understood. The answers, on the contrary, *though certain*, were neither so quickly obtained nor so easily unravelled. But the priests and magicians, who had been taught in the labyrinth of the temple how to understand the voice of the gods, the answers of the planets, the language of birds, serpents, &c., *easily* understood *the dead*, and became the interpreters. The priests reduced this to an art, whose most necessary *point*, and that which was best suited to the dead, was *absolute* silence, *silence and darkness*. They retired into deep caves, they fasted and partook of the soporific cakes (*panis frugibus*), and lay on the skins of sacrificed beasts. When the applicants awoke from the dreams, it was to reveal their most inward and secret thoughts. In fine, all the religious ceremonies of the Egyptians were directed to the knowledge of the *future*. Even these practices are resorted to by the ignorant to ascertain future events: a pretended conversing with the dead has always been a fruitful source of delusion and deception. Modern spiritualism is merely another phase of these ancient customs of a superstitious and ignorant people, who were the dupes of the priest, the magician, and the soothsayer. The priests of Egypt, Persia, China, Syria, and Hindostan pretended to bind the gods to their idols, and make them descend from heaven at their pleasure; they even threatened the sun and moon to reveal the secret mysteries and to shake the foundations of the heavens. *Vide* 6th Book of Virgil's "Æneid."

To the intelligently educated *the blind faith* with which the priests of China, India, Syria, and Egypt hold the hundreds of millions as slaves to their will and bidding, is hard to be understood. The great mass of the human family never think beyond their immediate necessities. The education received from their teachers is never questioned. "He that believeth not is damned" is the secret of a power the greatest ever exercised by man over his fellow-man. The disbeliever was hurled with all the anathemas into hell, which was painted as a region of misery and eternal torture. The initiation into the mysteries was a deliverance from the living death of vice, brutality, and misery, the beginning of a new life of reason, virtue, and happiness Moral and

VITAL AFFINITY.

divine axioms were inculcated and represented by all kinds of shows and allegorical performances.

With those who have perfect faith, a blind confidence, how easily is the brain acted on! Mental hallucination is so powerfully produced, that the delusion is as easily effected on a multitude as on a single individual. Do not at this day the priests of Buddha and Brahma produce miracles on the minds of millions who *never doubted?* The essential element to success is *faith*, implicit, blind *faith;* if the people were *to doubt*, no miracles could be produced!

There are elementary forces inherent to special forms of matter, which co-exist with it, when matter changes its form or the forces change their condition; so do we find different phases in the forms of organization, whether organic or inorganic. Light, heat, electricity, magnetism, vitality, are associated with matter in various proportions, giving it definite conditions. In organized matter, as exhibited in animal existence, it is these forces which in various combinations contribute to the functions of the animal economy. Does not the attractive and repulsive condition of matter depend on the relative states of its existence? What is chemical affinity but the preference of one body for another under certain conditions? Sulphuric acid $(S+O^3)$ will combine with magnesia, and so remain under favourable circumstances; but the moment it is brought in contact with lime or baryta, it leaves the one and combines with the other. The same laws are manifested in organic existences—there are positive inherent conditions, otherwise the particular forms of matter would not exist. Does not inorganic matter assume definite forms of crystallization? Is not the same principle exhibited in the structure of plants, as seen in the infinite variety of the leaves and flowers? It is therefore not asking too much of living matter that it should, in accordance with its specific character, produce definite forms. Surely that which we are obliged to admit as being the inherent property of inorganic substances, we cannot deny to superior organizations? Does not the same law of attraction and repulsion govern the planets, hundreds of millions of miles distant from each other? Was it not the disturbance of Uranus in its orbit which caused Leverrier to discover Neptune? Is the minutest or protozoic form of life less subject to these laws? Is it not the particular physical condition of the globe, our earth, which determines a corresponding development in organized beings on its surface?

Man, as a product of this planet, must follow and conform to its

VITAL DEVELOPMENT.

hereditary laws; it was these which brought him into being; it is by these that he continues to exist from age to age. From the first germ of vitality on the earth, a mere minute globule, through successive periods, gradual developments took place in accordance with the altered state of the earth itself. Until after vast stages of transitions man appeared, no doubt in a very inferior type; until now we find him investigating the composition of worlds, whose distance is incalculable, by means of the spectrum analysis, and with the same certainty as if the body were within his immediate grasp!

The warning star of the Egyptians, Sirius, a body a hundred times larger than our sun, whose distance is so great that its light takes sixteen years to reach our globe or suns twenty times the distance of Sirius, which is 143,000,000,000,000 of miles distant, are brought on the investigator's table and scrutinized. On the earth itself, the fact of holding intellectual intercourse across oceans and continents with greater rapidity than the world itself revolves on its axis, are marvels which put to the blush all the wonderful works of the ancient priests. Science is the great educator of the human race. She never retrogrades; her advance is steady but sure; she is the cause of truth, and must prevail. The veil of error once raised, ever after it remains exposed to the eternal light of scientific truth.

CHAPTER VIII.

DREAMS AND ABNORMAL BRAIN AND VITAL FUNCTION.

DREAMS are at all times shadowy, and easily fade away; there are some, however, which for a short time produce a marked impression. Dreams are sometimes so fascinatingly delusive, that we are chagrined at their sudden or abrupt termination, and desire their continuance. That this should take place, the brain must be thrown into a corresponding condition to that in which the dream took place, otherwise no continuation can follow. Some persons of great *will* power can throw themselves into this dreamy condition, and indulge for hours in the wildest fantastic delusions. This semi-sleepy, dreamy state is that known as "castle-building:" when all the sense of reality is experienced in this delightful reverie, we love the deception and correspondingly hate the bitter truths of life. Is it not the extra cup which exhilarates the brain function, and makes all appear "couleur de rose"?

Alcoholic excitement in some is a delirium of pleasure which is never experienced in the normal state: that is, the brain of some is naturally so sluggish or so torpid, that in order to experience pleasurable emotions a stimulant must be resorted to. Herein consists the danger of over-indulgence; "we drown our cares at the expense of life and health;" for the dose has to be constantly augmented in order to produce like effects. Habitual use negatives the original effect; it necessitates a constant addition to reproduce "the glorious forgetfulness."

We are naturally most uncharitable in denouncing the man who enjoys *a new existence* during this artificial state of excitement. Those whose brain function is always adequate to mental manifestation, cannot understand the intense pleasures and brain-power produced by resorting to stimulants.

When the brain is in perfect repose or sleep, no dreaming takes place. This condition is only possible when one or more portions of the cerebral mass are in a state of activity. The incongruity or consistency of the dream will depend on the parts of the brain brought

DREAMS.

into action during the dream. We cannot correct the absurdity, no matter how irrational; it is believed to be the truth, the impression sometimes remaining for some moments after awaking to perfect consciousness. Those portions of the brain which correct the delusive impressions are asleep. It is this identical state of brain *represented by blind faith;* the reasoning faculties are not exercised. Here consists the power of the priests of Buddha or Brahma over the minds of the people; their brains from the earliest period of existence having been tutored to take for granted the dogmas of the creed of their ancestors, they dream when awake, and in FULL FAITH BELIEVE THE DREAM, because the reasoning faculties have never been allowed to have independent exercise of their functions. Their standard has been limited to the artificial education of their priests.

No doubt the reader will bring to mind cases where the same influence exists in other countries than China, Hindostan, or Egypt, where the brain power of the priest arbitrarily thinks for the people; those who are strictly orthodox should never think for themselves.

The systematic dreamer regularly visits in his sleep his favourite country—a special creation of his brain. It has its forests, mountains, lakes, &c. He has established a double consciousness. He lives, as it were, in two worlds, and nightly visits, according to the state of his digestive organs, the ecstatic scenes of an ideal Elysium or the imaginary horrors of Tartarus. This dreaming state, according to its activity, influences the condition of the brain during the wakeful hours; or, conversely, our dreams are oftentimes shaped by the events of the day. Some dreams immediately preceding the waking state are so vivid, as the brain is then fully charged with nervous force or fluid, that its functions are performed with a rapidity which is inconceivable, if we measure them according to the standard of our waking thoughts; so that during the dream of a few seconds' duration, scenes and occurrences will pass in review with exact precision, as if it were the vista of a whole life, from our earliest childhood, all through the various stages of existence, depicted with faithfulness in all their original glorious reality; the reminiscences of the youthful brain are re-enjoyed in our dreams of after-life. In fine, the BRAIN LATENTLY retains every impression which has been presented to it through the senses; it only demands that a necessary condition should exist in order that the renewal to the original impression should be memorized. Loss of memory is the incapacity to reproduce this favourable state of brain. The very effort to memorize defeats the object sought, by calling into operation a portion of brain, at the expense of that portion which contains the information required. It is a principle of cerebral physiology, that when one portion is in active exercise the rest is in a comparatively negative state; the active function of the intellectual organs of the brain renders the animal dormant; or, conversely, if the animal has full control, the intellectual are rendered powerless.

Who could control a raving mob by an appeal to their reason? The paroxysm must be exhausted ere we can successfully treat the disease.

During the first stages of inhalation of the protoxide of nitrogen gas, ether, or chloroform, the brain is preternaturally excited by the sudden extra supply of nervous fluid from the lungs. During that stage its functional condition is similar to that of the vivid dream prior to waking. Then it is that the inhaler experiences the exquisite delirium. All the cares and ills of life are abolished in the temporary intoxication.

The highly constituted nervous condition of some brains is such, that the whole life is passed, as it were, in a dreamy state; whilst others, from an opposite constitution, being so sluggish and lymphatically apathetic, in order to realize the pleasures of mental excitement, are forced to have resort to stimulants.

Oftentimes when the brain is abnormally excited, as in fevers, the dreaming state may be so active that the senses become subservient to the delusions. The patient *believes* in the presence of things which have no existence: *he sees and hears* from his brain without the visual or auditory organs. No amount of persuasion will convince him that his room is not occupied by persons with whom he holds an imaginary, to him a real, conversation. During *delirium tremens* the same delusions and spectral illusions take place; the *brain's* abnormal activity is so great as to project the dreamy illusive condition, so that the patient *is haunted* with companions whose existence is only the result of irregular or disordered function. It was this diseased condition of brain, producing such deceptive images, which led to the discovery, by the author, of *Induced Mental Hallucination, or electro-biology;* a state of brain corresponding most faithfully to that just cited.

No matter how inconsistent, irrational, or incongruous the subject, it is believed most implicitly during the period of the brain's abnormally induced state to be the truth. *Vide* Mental Hallucination.

We come into the world with inherent organic predispositions: that is, our brains are fashioned to receive one class of things in preference to another; one brain, from heritage, climate, geographical position, has certain natural capacities which may not exist in another. It is

DREAMS.

not to be supposed that the primitive education or surroundings of our earliest days do not modify and shape our future modes of thought; it is impossible to master or entirely stamp out the impressions of early youth. These are the basis on which all brain function is subsequently associated.

A strong emotion or impression in after life, either of grief or joy, of such serious import as to disturb our domestic relationship, as the loss of a beloved parent, or the unexpected possession of fortune's favours, will often so indelibly be photographed on the brain as to become the permanent basis of our future dreams. It is these violent mental shocks which make such a lasting impression on the brain, so that the least disturbing cause during sleep will provoke the most horrid or the most ecstatic dreams, with a vividness and power which leaves the brain unconsciously depressed or exalted during the waking state. Sometimes when during the dream we have been *deceived* and tantalized in our dearest affections, and our most cherished hopes blighted and crushed, the brain is left in a state of nervous exhaustion, and it is with great difficulty that any mental effort demanding a high order of thought can be exercised by the brain until a restoration has been established by

"Nature's sweet restorer, balmy sleep;"

but it must be undisturbed by dreams.

The functional exercise of any organ demands the expenditure of nervous force or fluid; the completeness or efficacy of these functions is always regulated by the supply of this nervous fluid. A superabundant, as well as a deficient supply, is equally prejudicial to healthy function. In the one case we have aberrations, hallucinations, mania, neuralgia; in the other, lethargic mentality, or even idiocy.

The remarkable case given of Mr. Gourlay's continued sleeplessness is illustrative of the one, and that of Cornelius Vromann's continued sleep of the other; they are antagonistic states of the nervous system. What was at first an abnormal state, by constant use or habitude, becomes eventually a normal function; verifying the old adage, that "use is second nature."

The condition which at first would have endangered life itself, if suddenly applied, is repelled at first with abhorrence; but by constant and gradual use the organs establish and adapt their functional exercise; and there is an accommodation to the new condition which actually becomes by this constant use essential to existence; for if too suddenly abandoned, the most serious results may follow.

No matter how large and beautifully proportioned the brain, it must be adequately supplied with nervous fluid, otherwise its functions are sluggish, wanting in mental power. A small brain of good quality, well supplied with its executive element, is far superior to one of large dimensions of coarse structure with an insufficient supply. A large brain must be associated with correspondingly large lung capacity, not alone mere size, for the respiratory condition differs in persons of different temperament. It is not to be imagined that the possession of a large respiratory apparatus necessarily implies a corresponding power of producing nervous fluid; in persons of lymphatic temperament there is an absence of intensity which is characteristic of the nervo-sanguineous temperament.

Quality more than compensates for want of quantity; in fine, quantity is a decided disadvantage if unaccompanied by quality. Under no circumstances can a coarse textured brain compete with one whose fibres are fine and closely, compactly, and densely arranged.

The examination microscopically of over 100 brains of Negroes, Indians, Chinese, has shown that these in the various degrees of texture are inferior to the European; in comparing the brain of the pure Negro with that of the Turk, there is as much difference as between pine and boxwood; the one being loosely held together, whereas the fibres of the other are closely compacted.

All animal fibres differ in as marked a degree. Compare the fibres of some fish and the muscles of the vulture or the eagle. Still both serve for the locomotion of the animal.

The density, firmness, and fineness of the brain is a criterion, every other condition being equal, as a measure of mental power. As a rule, all parts of the body co-ordinate in point of quality; it seldom happens that a dense brain in health co-exists with flabby muscles.

A leading journal in writing of the crews of the University boat-race of 1871, says:—" The Oxford eight is manned by a heavy set of men, "powerful so far as mere strength is concerned. The Cambridge crew, " on the other hand, are devoid of roughness, compact and work well to-" gether; they never seem *distressed*, no matter what test they are put " to." This description exemplifies the difference between quantity and quality. No physiologist after reading this graphic description would have betted on Oxford; in fine, he would have given odds in favour of the *compact* Cambridge crew, which the result justified. The smaller crew had the quality of structure, which enabled them to sustain a prolonged effort without fatigue; thus endurance DOES NOT BELONG to mere size.

PRIMITIVE VITALITY.

Every state of brain exhibits its corresponding effects; every phase of existence, from the earliest period of childhood to decrepit old age, has a corresponding condition of brain. The eye of the eagle can gaze at the sun, but that of the owl is dazzled and blinded by its light. Still they are both visual organs, each adapted to the particular sphere of functional exercise. So with the brains of the various forms of living matter, from the simplest ganglion to that of the highest development in civilized man. It is evident that these developments have been consequent on the chemical or telluric state of the earth itself at the various stages of its existence; all the modifications of life are marked and defined in the various zones of the planet, which is continually undergoing changes. From this cause have been brought into existence the successive grades of organization. The lowest forms of life are not prejudiced by a higher state, fitted for the existence of superior organizations. These are found in all parts of the earth's surface, in the full exercise of their reproductive functions, as they were at the earliest periods. If, however, a lower condition or change should temporarily take place, then the higher would become extinct. As the changes of the earth's state of vitality have been inconceivably gradual, covering unnumbered ages, so have the distinct developments been brought into being, as distinct creations, each specially of its type, genus, order, or family. These may have been modified by the constant changes of the vital element emanating from the earth itself in combination with solar influence. There was a period when the *crustacea* alone could exist; so there was a time when the different types of monkey, according to the special zone, were brought into existence. No doubt this was immediately prior to the period when the lowest types of man had first a habitation on the globe. It may be that the earth's creative function, in the production of animal life, has passed. It is impossible for our faculties to define a state of creative function. But if under certain favourable combinations the minutest and most simple forms of life are now brought into existence, it is not unphilosophical to infer that the creative condition of nature, under correspondingly favourable states, could not have produced a mammoth or a whale.

CHAPTER IX.

VITAL PHOTOGRAPHY.

THE exquisitely sensitive condition of the nervous coat known as the retina, is such that it appreciates a vibratory movement of the one-trillionth part of an inch in a second. These vibrations of the molecules of the medium of light convey to the brain all the forms and conditions of the surrounding universe. The photographic impression on the sensorium is permanent or transitory, in accordance with the state of existing conditions. During the early periods of life, the brain is much more sensitive to impressions than in after-life. So permanent are these impressions, that they never can be effaced. They may be modified or toned down by after experience or education, still it is these first impressions of early youth which form the basis on which all our subsequent ideas are built.

The first are the most simple impressions; they are conveyed through the optic nerve, in the same vibratory manner, to the brain, which is constituted to receive the various images, and it is only by a reproduction of the identical vibratory state, that the conscious memory or the history of our *past experience is reproduced*.

It must be admitted, that as the external sense of vision is so sensitive as to receive the vibrations of colour or waves per second in a single inch of space without confusion, the brain itself, of which the eye is merely the servant, must at least be equally sensitive.

The following enormous numbers show the impulses per second on the retina:—

Extreme red	399,101,000,000,000
Soda yellow	509,069,000,000,000
Extreme violet	831,479,000,000,000

The only analogical approach to this sensitive state is the iodized silver plate to the action of light; it requires the minutest fraction of a second to impress an image. The vitalized electrical effects far transcend any of the purely chemical phenomena of which we are cognizant. The functions of the nervous system are so rapid, that they

VITAL PHOTOGRAPHY.

cannot be measured by any ideas we possess of time. There are states of nervous sensibility so great that permanent impressions take place from causes apparently the most remote.

No surface with which we are acquainted can compare in point of extreme sensitiveness with that of the child *in utero*, when it is surrounded with fluid, the liquor amnii. Then every shock or impression which affects the mother's brain is vibratorily conveyed to the child; that is, the fluid receives the shock, and these vibrations represent the forms or images of things taken in through the sense of vision. Under ordinary or normal states of the mother, these influences have not a marked effect, as there is no nervous connexion. It is only when the brain of the mother receives a *violent impression* that it is, as it were, reflected or thrown off, the consequence being that the whole system receives the shock, and that portion which is most sensitive, and in a manner independent, receives the image.

We know that the filaments of the auditory nerve are suspended in a liquor which vibrates or undulates more than 8000 times per second in conveying to the brain high notes of sound; so that here is an analogous condition to that in which the liquor amnii is thrown when the nervous system of the mother has received an impression so severe as to be thrown off from the brain.

It is not to be supposed that this vibratory condition of the fluid is limited to 8000 per second, it may be 8,000,000. But the fact of the fluids being instrumental in the conveyance of impressions, is here demonstrated as being a functional property of the animal economy. The transmission of an image to the brain through the sense of sight, is effected by the undulations of the ethereal medium, as exemplified in the action of light on the retina. The eye is a perfect camera obscura; the same arrangement of lenses, the identical mode of producing the picture. The choroid coat represents the ground glass on which the picture is focused, from which it is vibrated through the optic nerve to the brain, which is a mass of nervous molecules arranged in a fibrous form. It is the vibration of these molecules in their various combinations which produces THE THINKING POWER. THOUGHT is the motion of these particles of nervous matter charged with vitalized electricity. It must not be supposed that the eye alone is impressed with the sense of light; there are animal existences whose surface is so delicately and sentiently endowed that they are cognizant of light, though they possess no visual organs. These may even be capable or appreciating and detecting the forms and conditions of matter. For example, the skin of the proteus anguinus, is so delicate as to be affected painfully on exposure to light; it is also aware of the approach of other living matter at comparatively remote distances by the sense of touch. The fact of the existence of the picture on the retina, shows the necessity for its existence, such an embodiment of the object seen being essential to mental or brain vision. And when it is remembered how extremely rapidly these transitions take place, that light travels at the rate of 186,000 miles per second, and that the waves or vibrations of violet are on a single inch 70,555, we arrive at the enormous figures of 831,479,000,000,000 impulses on the retina in a second. It demonstrates a sensitiveness which we have no parallel to reason from. That numberless variety of movements or vibrations of the nervous molecules take place corresponding with the impression on the senses, it is impossible to doubt.

In fine, it is not a speculative conclusion that the brain must receive impressions from the senses in harmony with the physical vibrations of light, sound, taste, smell, and touch. In order to do so, its anatomical construction must be such as to respond to these vibratory communications and impressions.

Memory is the reproduction of the vibratory configuration representing the original images conveyed to the brain. It is the combination and recombination of these vibratory movements which produce *thought*.

The simple elementary forms are first received: these in course of time, according to the cerebral capacity, are compounded until the individual has attained by educational experience sufficient information to use the highest brain function, namely, of knowing the relations between cause and effect.

There are other conditions necessary in order that the brain function should be exercised with power—the supply of nervous fluid by the lungs must be adequate to the expenditure.

It has been shown that some persons resort to stimulants in order to excite brain function in consequence of a natural sluggishness. This abnormal excitement, though at first it may be attended with beneficial results, ultimately destroys the mental powers, as constantly increased doses are demanded in order to produce like effects.

When the anæsthetics are inhaled, the productive function of the lungs is so great, and the supply to the brain so sudden, that a *nervous congestive state* is the consequence. If, however, small quantities are inhaled, there is merely an exciting or stimulation of the cerebral functions. The most effective stimulating vapours are those which act on the nervous filaments of the lungs, exciting them to increased functional action in the production of the nervo-vital fluid. In

VITAL PHOTOGRAPHY.

this particular none surpass the action of protoxide of nitrogen. It has this most important advantage, that it does not interfere with or destroy the composition of the blood, which is invariably the case when the chlorine and carbon compounds are inhaled. It is true that the venous blood is prevented in a great measure from throwing off its carbon with freedom, in consequence of the increased action of the nervous tissue contracting the mouths of the venous capillaries. This is, however, a condition which must exist with all anæsthetics which act promptly on the brain in producing nervous congestion. The nitrous oxide does not destroy the nervo-muscular tone of the heart, which is always liable to be paralysed in the inhalation of the chlorine and carbon anæsthetics. All substances which have a tendency to disintegrate the natural component parts of the blood should be avoided. When the vitiated blood comes in contact with the walls of the heart, it negatives the nervous influence derived from the cardiac plexus. If it does not suspend its contractile powers, it oftentimes lays the foundation of future morbid functional derangement.

We must now re-occupy ourselves with the consideration of *Vital Photography*.

There is abundant evidence that the nervous vibratory shock of the mother is communicated to the body of the child, conveying under favourable conditions, a faithful embodiment of the impression which has caused such an emotional paroxysm. When the Egyptian magician was asked what class of persons were susceptible to the action of the narcotic fumes, he replied, "A boy under puberty, a "virgin, a black female slave, and a pregnant woman."

It is well known that during the early periods of pregnancy some women are peculiarly susceptible to influences which do not affect them at other times; the whole nervous system seems to be thrown into a state of abnormal excitement. During this period, any powerful mental shock will be conveyed to the fœtus.

The following cases will exhibit how the nervous vibratory configurations are conveyed from the brain to the liquor amnii, and thence to the sensitive nervous surface of the child.

Case 1.—Whilst in Grass Valley, Nevada County, California, in 1852, General G. showed the author the representation or counterpart of a large green snake which encircled his body. The explanation of this phenomenon was that his mother when four months pregnant with the General, was present when one of the negroes on the plantation, having killed a snake, had put it round his waist in bravado. On Madame G. seeing this, she was so powerfully impressed as to swoon or lose consciousness, and on the birth of the child, the figure of the snake was found to be not only photographed, but embodied on the child. It is a curious fact, that in the spring of the year, when these snakes recover from a state of torpor in which they remain during the winter months, the snake impression on the General increased in size and rotundity, and assumed a vivid green colour, which disappeared during the autumn and winter months.

Case 2.—A lady during the fourth month of pregnancy saw a large Newfoundland dog destroy a lamb. On the birth of the child it had a sheep's countenance, and a plentiful growth of wool on the back.

Case 3.—In crossing the American plains (1850) from the Atlanic to the Pacific coast, a lady who was pregnant had ridden on a mule for over four months. A short time after delivery in San Francisco, the right arm of the child was continually in motion, as if in the act of using a whip, which corresponded with the motion of the mother's arm during her pregnancy, flogging the mule. This movement continued for two years.

Case 4.—A pregnant woman, in Deptford, was frightened by a monkey. On giving birth, the child's face was an exact counterpart of the animal. The shock on the poor woman was such, that in two subsequent confinements her children had the monkey physiognomy. Injuries to the nervous system are often propagated.

Case 5.—A woman in the third month of pregnancy was frightened by a large black dog playfully jumping on her. The shock was so great that in a few weeks subsequent she miscarried, the fœtus having the head of a dog.

Case 6.—A lady in the second month of pregnancy was frightened so much as to be deprived of consciousness, in consequence of a mouse jumping on her shoulder from a cupboard. On the birth of the child, the prototype of the mouse was embodied on the shoulder.

A strong desire, or longing unsatisfied in a pregnant woman, will oftentimes be impressed on the offspring.

Case 7.—My own brother has a salmon depicted on his thigh. The miniature fish is complete, even to the colour, which is particularly vivid during the period this fish is in season.

Brain shocks are productive of the same results in the lower animals.

In June, 1870, at the country seat of Mr. Ellmore, near Calais, a favourite rabbit, which had been reared in an unoccupied stable or out-house, was frightened by the entrance of a sheep. In littering

VITAL PHOTOGRAPHY.

some twenty-five days after, one of the young rabbits had a sheep's head.

Another case is that of a sow, who, being alarmed at the sight of an elephant, gave birth to a young pig, with an elephant's head, with proboscis complete. This *lusus naturæ* was a Cyclops, having only one eye in the centre of the forehead. The specimen is in the Museum of the Paris School of Medicine.

The following letter from Dr. H. Garasse, of Calais, will explain :—

"En Juin, 1870, dans un château des environs de Calais, est un
" phénomène très curieux que est la plus belle preuve du système écrite
" par le très honorable Dr. Collyer, 'la Photographie Vitale.' Une
" femelle des lapins, pleine depuis quelques jours, fut enfermé pendant
" un temps de pluie dans une étable; quelques minutes après fut in-
" troduit un jeune mouton. La femelle du lapin en eut une telle frayeur
" qu'elle jeta des cris, se précipita contre les murs, et faillit se tuer. On
" retira le mouton. Vingt-cinq jours après cette frayeur extrême, elle mit
" bas sept petits, le septième présentant une tête de mouton et l'arrière
" tronc du lapin. J'affirme sur l'honneur la véracité de ce fait, et j'en
" remets au Dr. Collyer la preuve de l'affaire.

" Un autre fait tout aussi curieux.

" On avait débarque à Calais deux éléphants venant de Londres
" pour le Jardin des Plantes de Paris. Une femelle de porc (pleine)
" en eut une frayeur telle qu'elle mit bas onze petites, dont le dernière
" portait une trompe et les oreilles de l'éléphant. J'ai donné ce phé-
" nomène à Monsieur Marssiat directeur de l'Ecole de Médecine de
" Paris, 1851.

"DR. H. GARASSE.

"Calais, le 31 Décembre, 1870."

This specimen of the rabbit is in the possession of Dr. Collyer, who will be pleased to exhibit it to those interested.

Numerous other cases might be cited, showing every degree of "mental shock" being thrown by the vibratory action of the nervous molecules from the brain of the mother to the body of the offspring.

This brain transfer or embodiment, is represented in all the operations of *thought*. Memory is the awakening to activity of the original vibratory configurations; an accidental word, a particular odour, a sight, will cause the reminiscence of scenes and things long since thought to have been forgotten. The most insignificant occurrence will cause the brain to revert to a host of associations; it only requires that the original vibratory cord should be touched, in order to review the past with all the vividness of reality. In dreams this state of brain is often present.

The case of Louise Lateau, reported by Dr. Lefebre of the University of Louvain, Belgium, where the stigmata represented the conditions of the crucifixion, bleeding from the hands, feet, and forehead, is easily explained by the physiological power of the brain over the rest of the body.

Some persons have the power of mental abstraction to such an extent as to produce local effects; this condition is much favoured if accompanied by the condition of brain which is described as *blind faith*; it is *vital photography self-induced*. There are hosts of similar cases of stigmatization or marks on the body, produced by the continued action of the brain. In fine, as this organ is the grand seat of the whole nervous system from which all parts of the body are supplied *with voluntary motion and sensation*, it is not astonishing that its continued undivided action, when directed to a special part of the body, should produce these results—*the embodiment of the brain impression*. This state of brain would be more effective if an hereditary predisposition had been received from a powerful mental abstraction of the mother during her pregnancy.

Many cases are on record in which actual *stigmatizations* took place from the *blind faith* of the person subjugated by the will power. On one occasion a coin was imaginatively rendered *red hot;* the mark of the burning took place. So when a piece of wood was mentally converted into a piece of *ice, a chilblain* followed. *Vide Original Experiments, Liverpool Mail* and *Standard*, October, 1843.

The author of these pages was the discoverer of the mode of inducing the state of brain known as " Electro-biology ; " which should be called " Induced Mental Hallucination."

The laws of light and sound are coeval with the existence of matter itself; light is a property which permeates all matter. Our senses being formed for the conveyance of impressions to the brain in accordance with the properties or laws of light and sound, it follows that there must be perfect co-ordination or harmony. It is a question as to whether these vibratory states do not modify or give character to forms of matter. No part of the animal economy is an exception to the laws which surround us; that is, all functional exercise must be, in health, in conformity to these laws. Motion is as essential to the *thinking* power as it is to the existence of life. A cessation of motion is the paralysis of the one and the death of the other.

Each thought has its corresponding arrangement or configuration of nervous molecules: except these vibrations can be brought into operation the brain is inadequate to mental function.

The propagation of deformities or diseased states through many generations, is only to be accounted for by the vibratory condition of the mother's nervous system being conveyed to the child during the early periods of gestation.

What is chemical action but a specific vibratory condition of the particles of matter? What is sensation, motor power, but a special vibratory state of the nervous fluid supplying the organ? How do the kidneys secret uric acid, the liver bile, the stomach gastric juice, each having a distinct chemical character, none of which are found in the blood from which the secretion is effected, if it is not through the nervous influence? It is the disturbance of these nervous vibrations in their functional exercise which causes a diseased condition of the organs. All organic matter has a special vibratory condition; our sympathies or antipathies depend on the unison or discord of these vibrations. Who knows that it was not this electro-chemical vibratory condition of the earth, at the various stages of its development, that did not *bring forth* corresponding creations, from the simplest molecular germ to the highest nervous organization, as represented in man?

CHAPTER X.

CREATIVE FUNCTION.

NATURE never contradicts herself; she has established a universal law that all matter, organic as well as inorganic, commences from a point or germ in the crystallization of the material of which the earth itself is composed. The process commences from the aggregation of a few particles, until the whole mass assumes its definite characteristic configuration. In the organic there is invariably an ovum, a *punctum saliens*, from which the parts are gradually accumulated until the future animal has assumed its definite condition to sustain independent life. The seed, which is the germ of the future plant, undergoes a similar process. It is thus, by the gradual addition of new parts that the animal chain is raised from the lowest forms of life, to that of the highest mammals.

The most perfect illustration of this principle or law, is that the analogous ovum exists in all animals. No microscopic examination can demonstrate a distinctive peculiarity *in the ovum of the frog* or in that which will form the future man.

In the uterus of all the mammalia every shade of development takes place, from the simple molecule, which day by day becomes more complicated, until the future being has evolved all the parts essential to maintain existence in conformity with the parent animal.

It is most difficult to imagine how a specific type of animal existence could emerge into one, equally distinct, of a higher state; *à priori*, it would occur that the condition that would change the one would equally transpose the whole. How could superiority of physical structure alone cause such an evolution? The smaller animals are equally perfect, and are as prolific as the larger. Size is merely an accidental physical condition. It does not of itself warrant the supposition that because of this condition *per se*, another or higher class could emerge solely from sexual causes.

No one who examines an ordinary fowl egg can discover the rudiments of the future animal. Still, by the mere application of heat, an evolution takes place, until bones, bloodvessels, nerves, brain; in fine, all the organs of the perfect fowl are formed. In this simplest of all processes—the mere continuance of a temperature about 60° Fahrenheit—all the necessary conditions exist. But it must not be forgotten that this egg had first to be matured in the body of the fowl; her vitality had communicated the condition of future life. The eggs or ova of animals of different orders are in this incipient stage apparently alike. The egg of the crocodile and that of the turkey, the ostrich, or the turtle, have no great difference in their component parts. Still, on being acted on by caloric, they bring forth creatures of the most dissimilar conformation and habits in conformity with the parent animal.

It is certainly the most natural supposition that the animal chain should have ascended from the simplest forms of existence, as seen in the Ascidian, which possesses the rudiments of a *chorda dorsalis*, so to speak. But where is the necessity of this special evolution, when an *ovum* possessing to all appearance the identical characteristics is developed into a distinct animal?

Does it not occur to those who advocate this doctrine, that if a condition existed that would cause a lower species to emerge into a higher, none of the lower would exist, or at least they would also be converted into intermediate stages of a higher state of development? It is begging the whole question to imagine that the lower animals select a particular class for propagation; there is no evidence in confirmation that this is the case. If this were so, does it not follow that a portion of a specific class or type would be transmuted into a higher, leaving the other portion *in statu quo*?

We are driven to the necessity of admitting that particular portions of the earth became electro-chemically conditioned, so as to cause the evolution of a higher development of animal organization. In this respect it is equally as difficult to imagine, in an abstract sense, the development from the alligator to the dog, as from the dog to the monkey, or from the monkey to the lowest type of mankind. It is quite certain that these have an increased cerebral development.

That man has always been "the glory and wonder of the universe" is not the fact; he was for ages on ages a mere vagabond, itinerant wanderer, the most helpless and least noble of the animal kingdom. He could not compare with them in strength, in fleetness, in vision, in hearing, in smelling; in fine, he led a precarious, miserable existence, as is now the case with low savage tribes.

The Caribbean Indian, the Bosjesmen, Mandans, Australians, the natives of the Society Islands, are appropriate types of the human

CREATIVE FUNCTION.

family which lived and flourished in low states of the "vital element," or conditions of the earth's electro-chemical vibrations, which at distant periods was not fitted for high mental development.

Intellectual man, in the few thousand years of historic knowledge, must be measured as if he were of yesterday. He has only *now* just commenced developing his *thinking faculties*. He was originally imitative and imaginative; exceptionally inductive or reasoning. Now we find him making application of his mentality or brain function to the purposes and prolongation of his well-being, the only rational mode of utilizing his superiority.

The application of steam and electricity to the purposes of life is a stride so gigantic, that all the Egyptians, Grecians, and Romans did in the zenith of their greatness sinks into insignificance in the comparison.

The annihilation of time and space may now entitle man to be "the glory and wonder of the universe."

It is impossible to measure time, in a geological sense, in millions or thousands of millions of years. All we know is, that at vast periods the most complete changes have taken place on the surface of our planet. In various stratifications we discover definite forms of animal existence, and these are uniform in all parts of the earth. It is not presuming too much in saying that these conditions were fitted for the organizations discovered and for none other. If therefore a special condition was only appropriate for an animal of a special development, why should not another condition be fitted for a higher? It was necessary that a lower condition of life should exist prior to a further advance in the animal chain. Did it necessarily follow that the advance was effected by an evolution or emergence from the lower? If we admit the theory that one class of animals could evolve from themselves another of higher development, we are forced to the conclusion that at remote epochs, in certain zones of the earth, the creative function existed from definite local electro-chemical or telluric states of the earth at those zones. This change must have been inconceivably gradual.

There are no sudden transformations; all the operations of nature are on a gigantic and grand scale, invariably commencing from the most simple forms, which are aggregated into the most complicated. Even in the highest organic structure represented by man, we discover in the *virile* fluid an essential element of future life, represented by a microscopic monad or vital molecule, with a caudal appendage, having distinct independent existence; in fine, *the lowest* form of organic

CREATIVE FUNCTION. 89

vitality being an essential element to propagate *the highest;* that too resembling a tadpole, only not being one thousandth the size. This sperm monad varies in different classes of animals, and unquestionably is a necessary existence in order to insure the propagation of the species. When the female frog has spawned, this seed would not *bring forth* if the male did not impregnate it. The same process with plants; it is necessary that the pollen of the male should impregnate the female, otherwise there is no fruit. Here we have the universal law exemplified in the necessary presence of the two forces, negative and positive, or the attractive and repulsive. No operation in the whole arcana of nature, from the most simple to the most comprehensive, but demands the active presence of these forces. Sterility, extinction, death, are the inevitable consequences when the forces cannot operate in unison; there are no products, no propagation of the species, and the race runs out.

Do not the seasons, on a large scale, represent this negative and positive principle, in the relative action of the solar influence on the earth, in accordance with its position?

In the spring of the year does not the *positive state* cause the sap to rise, the buds to come forth, the trees to be covered with leaves and flowers? The whole face of the vernal portion of the earth is decked in beauty and youthful vigour; at the same time the antipodean region is suffering the effect of a *negative state.*

The earth's magnetic state produces a direct effect on all the forms of creation, and materially modifies the powers or functions of reproduction. All bodies possess organized magnetism, and the phenomenon presented is in accordance with the special organization with which it is associated.

All forms of motion emanate from the operation of the two forces. It must be backward or forward, upwards or downwards, expansive or contracting; if there is a force to repel there must be one to attract.

All the forms and modifications that exist in the universe are the result of matter, force, and motion. The very component parts of the earth are a mixture of acids and alkalies. This condition enters largely into the composition of the vegetable and animal forms of matter, producing their alternate expansions and contractions. These mark the growth and decay of life; at the point where the attractive and contracting forces cease, the repelling and expansive forces commence. It is thus that the course of constant alternate destruction and reproduction is continued.

In conclusion, no one who attempts theorizing as to the origin of man or any other animal, must omit the fundamental principle, that

CREATIVE FUNCTION.

the earth's telluric or electro-chemical state at special periods must have played a most important part in the special creation.

There is a constant correlation or harmony of the laws which have been directly instrumental in bringing into existence these special organizations. They are repeated in the embryological development, in the metamorphosis of ovum into the larva, and thence into the pupa and butterfly.

It is, however, no more difficult to conceive a special creation than that a state should exist which would cause one species to evolve another higher than itself; still, that the condition which produced this evolution should not have supplanted or rendered extinct the original source or progenitors from which the evolution took place. This difficulty at first appears to be an insuperable argument in favour of the theory that the various developments were distinct and special creations, in accordance with the earth's generative state.

Even supposing this to have been the case, we do not overcome the absolute necessity that the germ or ovum of the superior organization demanded *a mother* or receptacle, wherein gestation should be gradually accomplished, and even after birth that the future being should be nurtured and protected during its early period of helplessness.

We are not driven from this fact to adopt the hypothesis, that our immediate progenitors belonged to the quadrumana or superior Simiadæ, which are now found on particular zones of the earth. It is more than probable that many important links in the zoological chain have been destroyed or become extinct. We have as many grades of the monkey as there are types of man, each possessing a particular geographical characteristic. Many lower types of man have disappeared, as also the animals which immediately preceded him.

In any case, we are forced to follow the natural law of production.

To imagine a perfectly matured being, created without having to pass through the various stages of embryonal development, infancy, manhood, is to deny the evidence of our experience, and to make the creation of man an exception to the rest of the natural laws which surround us. If man did exist exceptionally as regards the laws which are essential to the rest of the animal world, then he might have had an exceptional creation; but we find him subject to all the contingencies and vicissitudes of the elements, like the lowest organizations. He only exists so long as he obeys the laws common to all created things.

The struggle of life over untold ages has been the lot of man. He has had to battle continually in his primate condition, not only with the

CREATIVE FUNCTION. 91

elements; he had to seek refuge in caves and places inaccessible to the numerous powerful carnivora. Savage in his nature, he destroyed his own kind, or those closely resembling himself. At this period he did not possess the faculty of speech, except to the most limited extent.

It can be conceived how man, in this early period, should have occupied his whole *thought* with the preservation of his existence. His natural *inherent* faculties were brought into functional exercise by the imperative necessities with which he was surrounded. In this state he would have remained to the present hour, had not the physical condition of the earth itself become more favourable for his advance and development.

It is a notorious fact, that certain zones of the earth are at this day favourable for the healthy condition of specific races, who if they change locality become the victims of disease and early death. If this is the case at this period of the earth's existence, it is not difficult to imagine a state when even greater chemico-electrical changes were taking place, *not suddenly*, in a few centuries, but covering millions of years; that man *in certain zones* was advanced in development, whilst others remained in the original state, whose zone of habitation was not similarly influenced. It is thus that we may account for the different races of man on the earth, whose physical characteristics are so pronounced that it is impossible to imagine that they ever originated from a single germ.

If we, however, admit the potent influence of the telluric or chemico-electric vibrations of the earth's "vital element" at particular zones, in combination with solar influence, and that man as a creature of the earth has been no exception to the rest of the universe, but brought into existence and developed in accordance with the creative function of the earth itself in special zones, we may reconcile and be enabled to account for apparent discrepancies and contradictions.

Whatever hypothesis is resorted to in the attempt to explain the original of man, it must essentially be surrounded with difficulties of such magnitude as to render the investigation one which will call forth all grades of criticism—from the pigmy critic, who indulges in invectives; the sectarian critic, who enlarges in a vainglorious style on "The ruler of the universe;" the pompous critic, who fancies himself a representative of man—"the wonder and glory of the universe;" the sarcastic critic, whose funny brain cannot get beyond the jellyfish; lastly, the gigantic critic, who mixes adroitly philosophy, science, and nonsense: *this is powerful*, as it carries the public mind.

CHAPTER XI.

FAITH AND WILL.

THE first periods of life are purely automatic: there is no established connexion between the voluntary function of the brain and the motor nerves, as these arise from the anterior portion of the spinal cord, which is a continuation of the anterior lobes of the brain, the seat of *the will.*

The earliest act of life *is the respiratory*, or the function of generating the nervo-vital fluid. Until this has been fulfilled the brain has no functional capacity, nor would the nervous fluid be of any service prior to that period, as the function of the senses could not be exercised. That there are movements of the child *in utero* cannot be doubted; these arise from sympathy with the mother through the circulation, as there is no nervous connexion, not a filament of a nerve being discoverable in the umbilical cord.

After the brain has established its *primitive function*, that of being the reservoir of the nervo-vital fluid, the child faintly commences to recognise light and sound. After some time acts of volition are attempted. It is astonishing how differently, as regards the time after birth, these acts occur in different children. In some the function is developed in a few weeks, whilst in others it requires as many months.

In the first great act of volition, *walking*, the whole undivided attention or direction of will is absolutely necessary, and also *the confidence* or faith of the child to use the muscles. Except these conditions of brain *will and faith* act in concert, the executive power cannot be exercised.

When confidence or faith has been once established, the *will power* is enabled to direct the nervo-vital fluid to the muscles of locomotion. Should, however, in these early trials, any circumstance occur to distract the child's attention, the act of walking is defeated.

After some time there is no difficulty experienced, for without any *apparent* conscious exertion of will, the muscles are directed by the

FAITH AND WILL.

brain. At least in after years we walk, talk, and exercise our senses to their fullest extent without any special effort of the will, so perfectly has the relationship been established.

The choice of action or discretionary will power is exercised by most animals, the sphere of its operation being in accordance with the special organization.

As a rule there is economy of the nervo-vital fluid; that is, no more is conveyed to the muscles than is necessary for the performance demanded, as in walking, running, or any other act connected with locomotion. If the expenditure is more than is actually required, exhaustion soon follows.

It has been shown that the gymnotus electricus at the will of the animal discharges from its nervous reservoir sufficient electric fluid to subserve the purposes of existence. In killing fish, if this act is too often repeated, the exhaustion is so great that it cannot escape being captured.

Whenever we desire to raise a weight, we employ a will power in accordance with the supposed strength required. No one in raising one pound would use the same condition of will as if he were to raise a hundred pounds. Conversely, if a piece of cork weighing one pound were so made *as to exactly represent* a piece of iron of one hundred pounds, and we exercised a will power of the muscles to raise a hundred pounds, whereas only one pound was raised, we should receive a shock so violent as to produce a recoil injurious to our muscular and nervous system; in fine, there would have been a useless expenditure of ninety-nine pounds of *will power*. Many of the most serious abnormal conditions of the nervous system arise from the irregular exercise of the muscles, or the deficiency in the proper government of the will in throwing out an undue amount of nervous fluid.

In raising one hundred pounds weight the whole force of a man's will is required. We are then exactly in the identical condition of the child in the first act of walking. We cannot afford to think and talk, as the whole brain attention is demanded in directing the nervous fluid to the muscles required to raise the weight, which may be one hundred or two hundred pounds, in accordance with the strength of the person.

The condition of the muscles in raising any weight is that they are charged with this nervo-vital fluid, which is discharged from the brain under the direction of *the will* in accordance with the force necessary to be exerted. If the brain has been much exhausted by the exercise of muscular exertion, so as to have produced the sense of fatigue, in order then to restore its normal functional condition, repose or sleep is requisite, when the lungs are specially called into action in regenerating the supply of nervous fluid.

The power of the will in the ordinary normal state is confined to the immediate acts essential to the functions of life; but it may be educated so as to be directed out of or beyond its ordinary channel. So that brain phenomena or abnormal states may be induced at the will of the individual, in order to arrive at a perfect control over organs not normally under the influence of *the will*, much time and constant habitude from an early age is required. It is this training of a specific exercise of the *will power* which is productive of cerebral phenomena of the most astounding nature, if viewed from the standard of the ordinary normal function.

It cannot be doubted that the energy of will used to raise one hundred pounds throws from the brain nervo-vital fluid adequate to that effort of the muscles. But suppose no weight is raised, and the same state of will is exercised, cannot the nervo-vital fluid be imparted *to other forms of matter*, producing results which, if not analysed critically, appear to the "uninitiated" as so marvellous as to be classed with the "supernatural?" That bodies possess latent vitality, latent electricity, latent light, latent heat, is unquestionable.

There is a religious caste in India (the Fakirs) who transmit to those of their children who are capable of exerting *great will power* the faculty of so directing *the vitalized electricity*, by constant educated use from their earliest age, as produce effects on inanimate matter which are *marvellous*. No doubt the celebrated feat of causing a plant to pass through all the stages of germination, from the seed even to fructification (which cannot be legerdemain, as it demands from three to four hours for its accomplishment), is the management and direction of the vital element under strong individual *will power*.

The vital element is used in all the functions of existence. Its great reservoir is the brain, from which, under the direction of the will power—if specially educated—it may be conveyed so as to impregnate inanimate matter. The following important experiment, often repeated by the author in 1842 and 1843, places the matter beyond speculation, in showing that there is an actual fluid thrown off from the nerves which changes the property of inanimate matter.

"Needles rendered magnetic by the nervous fluid."

The *Comptes Rendus* for January 2nd, 1838, contain the following, communicated to the French Academy by M. Becquerel from a letter received from M. De la Rive:—

"Dr. Prevost of Geneva has succeeded in magnetizing very delicate soft iron needles by placing them near to the nerves, and perpendicular to the direction which he supposed the electric current took. The magnetizing took place at the moment when on irritating the spinal marrow a muscular contraction was effected in the animal."

The irritation of the anterior portion of the spinal cord threw the muscles into spasms or sudden contractions, independent of the will of the animal. The same result took place as when *the will* was exercised to raise one hundred pounds, when the actual expenditure necessary was only for one pound. This extra will power of ninety-nine pounds would not only magnetize soft iron needles, but also impregnate other forms and conditions of matter, giving it properties and rendering it capable of functions which appear mysterious without a knowledge of this transfer of the vital element.

Sir David Brewster, in his Letters on Natural Magic, addressed to Sir Walter Scott, says:—

" One of the most remarkable and *inexplicable* experiments relative to the strength of the human frame, which you have yourself seen and admired, is that in which a man is raised with the greatest facility, on *the instant that his own lungs and those who raise him are inflated with air*. This experiment was, I believe, first shown in England a few years ago by Major H., who saw it performed in a large party at Venice under the direction of an officer of the American Navy. As Major H. performed it more than once in my presence, I shall describe as near as possible the method which he prescribed. The heaviest person in the party lies down on two chairs, his legs being supported by the one and back by the other. Four persons, one at each leg and one at each shoulder, then try to raise him, and find his dead weight to be very great from the difficulty they have in supporting him. When he is replaced on the chairs, each of the four persons takes hold of the body as before, and the person to be raised gives two signals by clapping his hands. At the first signal he himself and the four lifters begin to draw a long and full breath, and when the inhalation is completed or the lungs filled, the second signal is given for raising the person from the chairs. To his own surprise and that of his bearers, he rises with the greatest facility, as if he were no heavier than a feather. On several occasions I have observed that when one of the bearers performs his part ill, as by making the inhalation out of time, the part of the body which he tries to raise is, as it were, left behind. As you have repeatedly seen this experiment, and performed the part both of the

"load and the bearer, you can testify how remarkable the effects
"appear to all parties, and how complete is the conviction that either
"the load has been lightened or the bearer strengthened by the pre-
"scribed process.

"At Venice the experiment was performed in a much more impos-
"ing manner. The heaviest man in the party was raised and supported
"upon the points of the forefingers of six persons. Major H. declared
"that the experiment would not succeed if the person lifted were
"placed on a board, and the strength of the individuals applied to the
"board. He conceived it necessary that the bearers should communi-
"cate directly with the body to be raised. I have not had an oppor-
"tunity of making any experiments relative to these curious facts;
"but whether the general effect is an illusion, or the result of known
"or of new principles, the subject merits a careful investigation."

There is no illusion; this experiment has been repeated a hundred times by the writer. All that is requisite to success is a combined effort of *will power*. It is the *concentration* of the will of the bearers with that of the person to be raised which, during the concentration of the will, throws the vital element into his body. In fine, the combined exertion of *will power*, though it is used (without muscular exertion) through the medium of the finger, is more than requisite to raise a weight of 500 pounds. The muscle is the MERE INSTRUMENT OF THE WILL—it has NO POWER OF ITSELF.

It must be observed that when the inspiration or inhalation was complete, the *raising* took place. The object of the inhalation was to fix and concentrate the *will power;* it demands an undivided act of *direction and attention* to the object. Any distraction or diversion will be followed by failure. "He who hesitates is lost." It is a most disastrous and weak state of brain *when confidence* has been lost; the irresolution which invariably follows leads to failure; it is equally true nationally as individually. The want of FAITH negatives WILL POWER. If these functions of brain do not act in harmony, no power can possibly follow. Combine, let them harmonize and act in perfect unison, and the most wonderful results are accomplished.

Half an hour prior to the death of a friend, the author took him out of bed. He was, so far as mere sense of weight is concerned, not heavier than twenty pounds; after his death he was "a dead weight" of 150 pounds. Why this difference? It was the loss of "the vital element."

The most powerful of all the forces known to man is the electrical when concentrated. Yet this very element is essential to our existence.

Cannot we here discover the secret of the phenomena of "table turning" and "spirit knocking?" There may be an imparting of the "vital element" or nervo-vital fluid, which under the *will power* or function of volition presented phenomena which, to those ignorant of this condition of the nervous system, were attributed to the "supernatural." In a future work this matter will be fully *discussed;* the author of these pages having been *the cause* of the ORIGIN of the subject known as "spiritualism," as recently developed.

The author in 1845 possessed an hydro-electric machine; the largest ever constructed. It was four times greater than that exhibited in the Polytechnic Institution of London, the experiments with which were so ably demonstrated by his friend Dr. George H. B. Bachhoffner. The huge battery of thirty-six Leyden jars of eighteen inches diameter and two feet high was charged from the machine in one minute. In those empty jars, from a mere disturbance of the equilibrium of the molecules of ethereal matter, was contained a power of momentous force; when the positive and negative surfaces were brought together, and in so doing made to pass through the brain of a large dog, its death was instantaneous. Yet *nothing was to be seen.* This electrical force was eliminated by the friction of dry steam through small tubes of hard wood. Yet this is not more wonderful than that a fish should generate electricity in water in *such quantities* as to kill its prey when directed by *the will* of (the gymnotus) the animal.

The torpedo, the silurus electricus, and the gymnotus are sensible when they have shocked an animal; nor will they exert their electrical powers when touched by an inanimate substance. This is a remarkable fact. The gymnotus has four electrical organs, which it may discharge separately or together: it can give two or three successive shocks, but if the prey has been stunned or killed by the first shock, it never discharges a second, but *economizes* its force.

The experiments of Wilson Philip in dividing the eighth pair of nerves, which put the stomach in direct communication with the brain, showed that when cut the digestive function ceased, but the moment the cut ends were united by means of a galvanic battery, the secretion of the gastric juices took place as perfectly as it did before the division of the nerves. Some persons immediately after dinner are overcome by an irresistible sleepiness. This arises from the digestive function depriving the brain of a large amount of nervous fluid, leaving the senses in a negative state. All these facts are adduced in order to show that the *nervous influence*, as it has been denominated, is closely allied to electricity, galvanism, and magnetism. The vital element when *secreted* by the respiratory organs, and retained in its reservoir, the brain, is conveyed to all parts of the body to subserve the vital functions; the major portion is, however, used under the direction of the will power, in *the thinking function of brain*, or the various muscular movements. The time is not far distant when these facts will be universally received. Until the physiology of the functions of the nervous system is better understood by the medical profession, the treatment of nervous disease will be futile, as it mostly is; from a deficient knowledge of this department of physiology it is, that these diseases are so difficult to treat successfully.

The exact government and direction of the nervo-vital fluid, so as to produce the greatest possible effect, is exemplified in those persons who have acquired "a knack," as it is called, in raising weights, or in striking a telling blow either with the hammer or the fist. It is by no means the strongest man who is capable of dealing the severest or heaviest blow. Acrobats and prize-fighters have this faculty of using the will so as to exert the greatest amount of force at a given time. On several occasions persons whilst waltzing have ruptured the fibres of the gastrocnemius muscle in consequence of the want of government of the will power. If the exertion was such as to produce ten times the muscular power required, there would necessarily be a too violent contraction of the muscle, inadequate to the motion required, and consequent rupture.

The history of neuralgic disease in its varied forms arises from the irregular distribution of the nervo-vital fluid—the seat of these diseases is in the brain—or from too abundant a supply from the lungs. At this moment a gentleman suffering the most severe form of sciatica is under treatment. In his case the disease has arisen from the brain having been for some thirty years actively employed in literary pursuits; the lungs having established a functional capacity to meet the demand. From a severe mental trial he discontinues his accustomed vocation. The brain not expending the nervous fluid generated, it finds expenditure through another channel, *the sciatic nerve*. The treatment consists in restoring the lost equilibrium. All those cases of epilepsy, neuralgia, hysteria, and trance indicate a local excess of nervous fluid; whereas paralysis is frequently the consequence of a deficient supply, or from over-exertion with an inadequate capacity, more particularly in the indulgence of the sexual propensity.* It is economy in the use of

---

* This subject of itself is so large and so replete with the most extraordinary physiological phenomena, that it must be reserved until a future occasion, when it will be specially treated in detail, in a work now preparing for publication, entitled "The Phenomena of the Vital Element Artificially Induced."

FAITH AND WILL.

VOLITION OR WILL POWER, and the maintenance of the equilibrium, which are the sources of continued health and longevity—*the source of happiness,* the aim of life.

UNBELIEF or loss of FAITH is one of the most extraordinary conditions of the brain, for when it exists all power of action ceases. The desire may be strong, but the power of execution so weak, that it is impossible to perform. The moment confidence is lost, and the power is called into question, that is sufficient; it is no use trying so long as that frame of mind exists. This loss of faith destroys the power to do. Over-anxiety, as well as *fear*, produces a loss of confidence.

The executive power, to be eminently successful, imperatively demands the presence of a united condition of faith and will. Once destroy, from whatever cause, the faith, and the power becomes weak.

If you fall several times on the ice, your faith has become so diminished that it is with great difficulty walking, under these circumstances, can take place without assistance. It is so in swimming; once lose faith or doubt your capacity, the power becomes weak accordingly. So it is in every act of life.

Nothing contributes so much to great national disasters as the lack of self-confidence. If, from whatever cause, there is once established in the mind of soldiers or sailors an impression as to the enemy's superiority, no matter whether well or ill founded, from that moment the chances of success are reduced. When once that peculiar condition of faith and self-confidence known as "the morale" is destroyed, the best of troops are rendered comparatively useless. It was the loss of confidence or "morale" caused by the terrible defeats at the commencement of the war, at Weissenbourg and Wörthe, which rendered the French army an easy foe to conquer. Its prestige was gone, and in the same ratio as it had lost confidence the German troops had gained. They no longer thought the French invincible. Success begets success; once impress the conviction that you are great, that you are powerful, everything else is taken for granted. If, however, by failure, irresolution, or hesitation, a policy of mere expediency is adopted exhibiting *weakness,* your prestige is lost from that moment. *Your influence, your power*, has CEASED TO EXIST. These great mental forces are nationally manifested each passing year. Knowledge is power. If the intellectual faculties of a nation are convinced that its armaments, discipline, and organization have been carried out according to the principles which scientific experience has proved to be the most powerful, both for offence and defence, this conviction will create an intellectual faith, and will result in the most extraordinary manifestation of will power. Faith based on the conviction of the intellectual reasoning faculties has a permanent and lasting hold on the mind; it is never subject to those frightful panics which invariably arise from ignorance; it sees a means to an end, and it is not easily discomfited by temporary reverses.

If soldiers once lose confidence in the intelligence of their leaders, that magic faith or united will power which has achieved all the great and brilliant triumphs of the past, cannot be exercised. It is this intellectual concert and harmony of mental states which conquers and annihilates all opposing forces. If these are not present, failure and defeat must be the inevitable result. Distrust your own powers and they actually cease. Whenever doubt, hesitation, or want of confidence takes the place of resolution, self-reliance, and a firm conviction of power, the will power is rendered negative.

France, prior to the war of 1870, was imagined to be the most powerful of nations, possessing complete armaments of the most improved description, her army and navy ready for any emergency. When, however, the hour of trial put her to the test, it was found that her condition resembled a mighty giant, or Samson, whom the Delilah of voluptuousness and corruption had lulled and betrayed into the fatal sleep of apathy, enervation, and false confidence. The total demoralization or want of discipline, and particularly intelligence, rendered her comparatively powerless. On the first reverses, caused by want of generalship or intellectual strategic action, she lost faith in herself: her strength from that instant had departed. It was "the cutting of the seven locks of hair;" it was then too late to cry, "the Teutons be upon thee, France," for her power of resistance had already become so weak that she had to submit to have her very eyes put out.

Disunited, discouraged in her helplessness, she became the mockery and the sport of the Teuton. Paris is fettered with an impenetrable barrier of steel guns. An enormous indemnity is exacted of 200 millions sterling, besides, "the unkindest cut of all," she is obliged to cede two of her most important provinces, that of Alsace and the greater portion of Lorraine. France, in blind frenzy, carries out the simile of Samson only so far as to commit the suicidal folly of a civil war, for she has not even the satisfaction of immolating with herself " the lords of the Philistines." "Whom the gods wish to destroy, they first drive mad."

France! you are eating the fruit of despotism and ignorance. Educate your children; then, and not till then, will they cease to be the sport of Utopian ideas, or the dupes of bigotry.

Your revenge is in the future; let it be one of high intelligence. One which will command the admiration of mankind. Your Gallic race has all the elements of intellectual greatness; only give it freedom of action. Unfetter your mercurial people; talk no more of ruling with "a rod of iron." Those fossilized ideas have in a very great measure been the cause of your present calamitous condition. So long as you cherish ignorance or despotism, so long will you be the sport of those nations who enjoy the high privilege of being *educated*, and though despotism will not allow them to act, they have at least the power *of thinking for themselves.*

Physical or brute force has no power *per se;* it, to have potency, must be under the guidance of knowledge. *It is the huge muscle* without the rational will power.

France, arouse from your torpor; come to intellectual, conscious life; throw off the incubus of Delilah, which has bound you in fetters. Remember the march of mind is onward. Those alone who can rule themselves have the faculty of ruling. The Goddess of Liberty has no sympathy with that chaotic monster whose attributes are a combination of despotism, ignorance, bigotry, and superstition.

Note.—The principal causes which tended to the extraordinary success of the Germans were—1st. Wonderful superiority of the artillery, which was employed with an efficiency, and at ranges never before known; 2nd. The automatic discipline and organization in every department of the army.

The writer having witnessed many of the battle fields in the late war, he is in a position to state how inferior is the military system of every other nation, when compared to that of Prussia.

CHAPTER XII.

MODERN SPIRITUALISM.

WHEN the scientific philosopher of the West revealed to the astonished Brahmin of the East some of the wonders of the minutest forms of the "vital element," of whose existence we should have for ever remained in ignorance had it not been for the invention of the microscope, the Oriental, instead of being delighted at the possession of knowledge which had been heretofore hidden from him, was rendered miserable, for the fundamental principle on which was based the most important feature of his religious dogma had been annihilated by the discovery of truth. The man whose faith had taught him to view every form of animated nature as something especially sacred, when convinced that he could not eat a fruit or drink a cupful of water without destroying myriads of creatures, visible by microscopic aid, possessing life and the powers of locomotion, with all the necessary organizations essential to both, the poor Oriental became from that moment an "unhappy man." Compelled to admit to himself that at every meal he was a destroyer, a devourer of animated beings; in fine, from his own moral standard, "a murderer."

It is not to be wondered that his existence became "darkened o'er with a cloud." All his hopes of a future elysium had been crushed, hopes cherished from his earliest days had been blighted. Instead of gratitude he inwardly cursed his Western friend who had so fatally, for his happiness, shown him the truth. We cannot even smile at the effect of the unwelcome knowledge forced on the unhappy Oriental, for it so forcibly reminds us that in our midst some of the most intelligent and educated show the same abhorrence at the revelation of any truth which destroys the dogmas of their peculiar belief. Ignorance with them, as with the Brahmin, is positively bliss. They shut their eyes to the light, and prefer the darkness, because the knowledge of the truth will cause their theories and speculations to vanish before the advance of scientific discovery.

The credulous, uninvestigating bigot would rather believe any proposition, no matter how preposterous, or contrary to the laws of nature, than a truth which does not harmonize with his doctrines. Tell him the pyramids of Egypt are on their apex, he will receive it so long as it does not antagonize with the dogmas he has cherished.

Newton's discovery of the true law of gravitation destroyed the philosophy of Aristotle, which had dominated for over two thousand years.

Galileo's discovery of the satellites of Jupiter, and of the revolution of our globe round the sun, upset ideas which caused his persecution by the blind and furious bigotry of the monks, who charged him with heresy. He was obliged to abjure and sign a denial, on which he stamped his foot, and said " yet it moves."

> " Truth crushed to earth will rise again,
> The eternal roll of years is hers ;
> But error, wounded, writhes in vain,
> And dies amidst its worshippers."

Dalton discovered that all bodies unite according to fixed and invariable proportions, on which he based his " Atomic Theory:" now chemistry is a mathematical science.

As the "vital element," when directed by concentrated volition, is capable of raising a man weighing two hundred or more pounds as if he were a *feather*, the question arises, if it is possible to communicate the "vital element" to inanimate matter, temporarily to impregnate a table or any other form of matter, so that, when so impregnated, it would be under the influence of the volition. The incongruity of the proposition ceases the moment we discover that on irritation of the spinal column, soft iron needles become magnetic, by the sudden concentration of the nervo-vital fluid.

My friend, the late Dr. Hare, Professor of Chemistry in the University of Pennsylvania, was convinced of the truth of *spiritualism* in consequence of *the movements* imparted to "a table" by what he thought "spiritual influence." If once the mind admits, or is convinced, that an effect arises from a specific cause, it matters not whether the inference was correct so long as *the conviction* exists. The effects are manifest, and cannot be accounted for by a mind which had been accustomed from its earliest days to the investigations of physical science. A table moves, and the movements actually make responses to questions proposed so naturally, that failing to discover a relation between cause and effect, the " supernatural" is called in to supply the deficient knowledge.

The writer must state some facts relative to the phenomena presented on these occasions.

Being in New York in 1853, at the Astor House Hotel, a party of six went to the rooms of a Mrs. Cohen, "a medium" of celebrity. On entering we paid each half a dollar and took our seats round a table. Mrs. Cohen requested that all persons present, who were not less than ten, should place their hands on the table; we had not done so more than five minutes when small sharp raps were heard. The alphabet was produced, when each person in rotation was allowed to ask two or three questions; as our turn came sixth, we had ample opportunity of investigating if any trickery existed; if such were possible. Those who preceded us mentally asked questions of the supposed spirits and invariably received correct replies. On coming to our turn, the person *thought of* had died in Sacramento a year previously. His name was distinctly spelt out. We then asked audibly what two objects did the deceased, or "did you give me," as we were supposed to address the deceased spirit. The answer was "a pipe and a pillow," which was correct.

It was not until the autumn of 1859 that another occasion offered to witness "a professional medium." On entering the apartment, we found several persons sitting round a table. On our taking a seat the number was seven. On an alphabet being produced, some replies were made correctly, while others were altogether wide of the truth. The "knocks" were heard on various parts of a table, and apparently on the sides of the room. It was at this time that the committee was formed, who, for the satisfaction of its members, made arrangements with the mediums to attend twice a week, the *séances* taking place at the respective residences of the committee.

On each occasion some unaccountable phenomena were presented; but we were soon led to suspect that the truth was so mixed with fraud and trickery that it was most difficult to assign which was the one or the other.

It was on the tenth *séance* that one of the committee, a clergyman, who was undergoing the *pinching operation*, seized suddenly the foot and secured the shoe. It was found that the fore part of the sole was removed, so that the toes could have free play. We have oftentimes seen people whose prehensile power with the toes was exercised with as great a dexterity as the fingers are ordinarily used.

This flagrant discovery of fraud had for a time a most prejudicial effect, as it naturally would on any person who was in search of truth.

Years passed away, when an opportunity was afforded of commanding a *vital battery*, that is of several persons, who were entirely ignorant of the phenomena. Our object was to discover the rudimentary fact, as to the possibility of an inanimate *substance* being charged with the vital element, so that when charged it would in a measure be under the influence of the will.

After the persons had placed their hands on the table for one hour and ten minutes, the table was so charged as to move or tilt, when *mentally* requested to do so. The vibrations which followed were remarkable and accompanied by the *cold current*. Since then we have had sounds produced, and on one occasion the most positive demonstration, where no deception was possible, that an object can be vitalized, and during the continuance of that state manifest phenomena which under ordinary conditions are only exhibited by independent life.

That abnormal phenomena connected with special conditions of the nervous system frequently occur, no one can doubt who has investigated the subject. The results are not uniform, nor can they be commanded, except the most favourable conditions exist for their manifestation. It is the many necessary conditions essential to success which render the investigation so difficult, more particularly with persons who will not understand that the nervo-vital phenomena cannot be measured or tested in accordance with our present knowledge of the physical laws which govern the natural sciences. Our limited experience has however indicated that if certain mental conditions are not observed, failure is the inevitable consequence.

The phenomena attendant on another phase of the same subject, animal magnetism, has shown that the state of the weather, mental harmony, or antagonism, have a most positive influence. The medium must necessarily be an extremely sensitive person, even morbidly so. How then is it possible that he can be calm, self-possessed, exercise mental concentration or will power, if he is rendered irritable, his sensitiveness wounded by purposeless opposition? It cannot be expected that if the essential conditions to success are destroyed that successful results will be produced. It would be as philosophical to break your watch and then express astonishment that it did not keep time. To be suspected of fraud when conscious of your honesty and truthfulness must be exceedingly mortifying to the sensitive medium.

The public, however, who are strangers to the extravagant pretensions of some of these spiritualists, who exercise their powers empirically, and who attribute the phenomena produced to supernatural agencies, must be pardoned for not giving credence to claims which are in opposition to all experience.

It is the necromantic portion of these manifestations which have brought discredit on the whole subject.

There is every reason to expect a rational solution without the intervention of spirituality. The correlative phenomena exhibited in somnambulism, unconscious cerebration, double consciousness, vital photography, spectral illusions (so-called), embodiment of thought, electro-biology—all furnish abundant material to explain the so-called spiritual manifestations.

The embodiment of thought is the cerebral representation or production of the figure thought of. If there is sufficient nervo-vital fluid at the command of the medium, he is enabled to produce an embodiment, which will for the time being, under the direction of the will power, manifest all the conditions of an independent existence. When the Fakir cerebrally produces the representation of a child, which is recognised by the spectators, no actual child is present, but a vital embodiment which, during the performance, possesses the attributes of life; it is a spectral illusion, in the sense that the visual organs recognise the palpable form of the child. It is a power only attained by constant exercise of the brain during a state of mental abstraction. It is also not to be expected that, with our limited space, the *rationale* can at present be given in detail. We must, however, admit that if the vital element can be accumulated in sufficient quantity, that a dominant will power would be enabled to use it so as to produce *the physical* phenomena, so to speak, of raps, sounds, or even music. We do know that in vital photography the impression on the child from the mother is not a mere picture of the object, but an actual *embodiment*.

There is a physical condition which invariably attends these manifestations, in the form of a cold current. We extract from a publication of our own, in 1862, February 1st, *Spiritual Magazine:*—

" One of the most remarkable conditions which accompany some of
" the highest and most complete manifestations of *spiritual* power is
" the presence of a *cold* current of air. This circumstance arrested my
" attention above twenty years since, when investigating the mesmeric
" phenomena. The coldness of the magnetized always occurred, and
" so great was the loss of heat in some cases that, except in the region
" of the heart, the surface appeared like that of a corpse. The phy-
" siologist should not neglect the opportunity of investigating the
" relation which these cold currents, whether nervous, magnetic, odic,
" or of some more ethereal atmosphere, bear to the phenomena."

These were our written ideas nine years since. In 1843, we published a work entitled *Psychography, or the Embodiment of Thought*. The subject is replete with intense interest, as explanatory on a philosophical basis of all the mysteries and miracles performed from the earliest periods of semi-civilized Babylon, Thebes, and Memphis, the miraculous performances of the ancient Grecians and Romans, to those of the Brahmins and Buddhist priests of the present day.

No matter how extraordinary the phenomena claimed by the spiritualists, the author is convinced that they are all susceptible of being explained on a philosophical basis, without resorting, or more properly, being driven to the *supernatural*, as the source from which these *apparently* mysterious phenomena originate. It demands a thorough knowledge of a special department of patho-physiology, or special information of the abnormal conditions, in their manifold phases of the nervous system, particularly somnambulism, hysterical coma, magnetic coma, epileptic coma, mental hallucination—in fine, brain functions in health and disease. Without this necessary knowledge no one is fitted to investigate these artificially induced nervous phenomena.

A man may be a profound astronomer, a proficient chemist, or the most able engineer, and yet totally incapable, from want of acquaintance with this special department of knowledge—which demands vast research to become conversant as to the characteristics and essential conditions—to be a successful investigator.

Our forthcoming work will cover the whole subject, and as we visit British India in a few months, much important information will be obtained amongst the Brahmin priests.

When the man mentioned by Sir David Brewster was raised at Venice on the points of the fingers of six persons, his weight did not appear to be more than that of a feather. As this experiment can be repeated by any one, its truth is beyond controversy. Now when the table is so charged, there is no difficulty in commanding its movements by mere cerebration. No doubt, all the real phenomena will admit of a physiological explanation without mystification. The whole subject of somnambulism, during which state there is a double consciousness, as of the stupid, awkward girl in her natural state, who when in the somnambulic state was possessed of the most remarkable powers, which could not be explained at the time, is being thoroughly investigated in connexion with other abnormal functions of the brain, showing that no matter how apparently mysterious the phenomena, in consequence of our ignorance of the laws of vitality, there is no occasion to attribute them to "supernatural" causes, as the mysteries are being unravelled, and its fogs dispersed by the light of scientific truth.

The late Professor Faraday found that the gymnotus electricus has four electric organs, which it could throw into operation either separately or together.

The gymnotus does not use the same amount of *will power* to stun or kill a *small fish* as for a *large one*. Nor does man use the same will power in raising one pound weight, as if the weight were one hundred pounds. This argument has been previously advanced; it is here repeated as being directly pertinent to the subject under consideration—namely, that it is the use of will power or volition identical with that exerted in raising a great weight, without exerting the muscles, which discharges, under direction of the will, the nervous fluid to any given object desired. The nervous congestive state known as mesmerism is thus induced in persons susceptible to the influence. The recipient being passive and the operator active, the former when reduced becomes, as it were, subject to the brain function of the latter. There is a remarkable instance recorded in the report of the Boston Committee (*vide* Appendix), where the chorea or St. Vitus's dance was transferred by the nervous atmosphere from the diseased boy to the healthy one, who was in the "nervous congestive state." The spasmodic involuntary twitchings of the muscles were as complete as if the disease had originated in his system. What may appear singular, the transmission took place at a distance of some thirty feet.

In the Japanese top trick the operator manipulates the wooden top some ten minutes, with undivided direction of *will power*, prior to the spinning, when the top is guided in every direction up and down at the will of the operator.

The object of this manipulation is to impart to the top the "vital element" or nervous fluid, wherewith once thoroughly impregnated, so to speak, it becomes subject to the will. The automatic direction of the will power of itself will not produce results; it must be accompanied by *blind faith*, which faith can only be attained as the result of long practice from the earliest age in persons of specific cerebral organization. If any *doubt* exists, or want of *confidence* even in a *minor* degree is manifested, the directive will power is seriously interfered with.

Amongst the Hindoos, Chinese, and Japanese, those of their children who at an early age manifest an aptitude in the exercise of great will power, are taught to exercise it; so that oftentimes they are not only enabled to produce the most extraordinary physiological results on themselves, but also to convey or impart to inanimate matter the nervous fluid. In fine, there is a great art in the concentration and direction of this "vital element."

The magnetizing of the soft iron needles by the nervous fluid is a case directly in point, as showing that there is a very close similarity in the properties of the nervous fluid and magnetism. It also demonstrates that inorganic matter may have imparted to it, from the organic, a condition which has entirely changed its properties.

It is so with the top of the Japanese. It is also the case *with the table* of the spiritualists; it becomes charged with "the nervous fluid" by the persons whose hands are placed on it, and whose brains are directed to the same object.

In the experiment of raising a man at the end of the fingers, it is absolutely necessary, to insure success, that all the bearers should act harmoniously; their volition must be simultaneous, otherwise failure is the consequence.

To those who desire to *recognise* by the sense of touch the nervous fluid, an experiment is easily performed to demonstrate its existence. A backward and forward movement of the hand rapidly made from the wrist, accompanied by great will power, will cause after a few seconds such an accumulation of *nervous fluid* in and about the hand, as to be distinctly discernible as *a ball*, appearing (if the eyes are closed) to be *solid to the feel*. Physiologically this is one of the most important experiments, as showing that this *nervous fluid* is thrown off from the brain and directed at will.

The reader must read this chapter in connexion with "Vital Photography," as the phenomena arise from the same cause.

When the subjects of "the nervous congestive state of brain," dreams, spectral illusions, vital photography, somnambulism, and induced mental hallucination are considered in connexion with the vital element and the power of *volition*, all the phenomena attributed to the marvellous or supernatural vanish as if before some magic wand, such is the mighty power of science, which, like the rod of Aaron, swallowed up all the other rods.

Had Dr. Hare, who was an eminent electrician, been able to understand the cause of the movements of the table, he would never have given credit to any of the phenomena which followed. It was the inexplicable movements of an inanimate object which upset the balance of an otherwise powerfully constituted mind. When once the Rubicon had been passed, the admission of unknown phenomena, which the disciples of "spiritualism" honestly enough no doubt ascribe to the supernatural because the phenomena were inexplicable, Dr. Hare, arguing on a purely philosophical basis, said, "Here are movements which make rational responses to my questions." He did *not* know that all the sensual impressions received from our earliest age remain *latent* in the brain, and that in order to render them *manifest* the necessary conditions have to be present. The case recorded by Abercrombie of the ignorant servant-girl who, during brain fever, repeated whole chapters in the original Greek of Homer, which she had *unconsciously* received on her brain from her master, a clergyman, who was accustomed to read Homer aloud, shows that during an abnormal state the brain's functions are so exalted as to astonish those who are unacquainted with the physiology of these phenomena.

When, however, we recognise the fact that inanimate matter not only receives the nervous fluid, but that its character becomes changed, as in the case of the soft iron needles, there is no difficulty in receiving the proposition that the table has had imparted to it, from the numerous persons having their hands placed on it, accompanied by their volition, the nervo-vital fluid, which is sufficient to account for the movements, for when once charged with the nervous atmosphere it becomes *subject* to will power.* When this fact is admitted, there is no necessity of ascribing the phenomena to spiritual causes.

Nothing is so prejudicial to the advance of truth as the denial of phenomena which exist, merely because they cannot at the moment be accounted for on known principles.

Those who investigate, as thousands will, the experiment of raising a body in the manner indicated by Sir David Brewster, will be forced to the conclusion, that the *power of volition* exerts a force which seems to overcome or counteract the laws of gravity.

---

* Nor is the NERVOUS INFLUENCE OR ATMOSPHERE confined to the uneducated. Some years since a Mr. Miller, commonly known as "Father Miller," was interpreting according to his version *Daniel's Dream*, which he pretended portrayed the immediate ending of the world in 1844. In Philadelphia, May, 1843, he had thousands of disciples, and others who out of curiosity attended his dissertations. On one occasion, Edgar A. Poe and the author attended where some 3000 persons were congregated. The excitement was intense, all seemed to think "Father Miller's" interpretation to be correct, and that *the end of the world was near at hand*. Miller entered into a variety of wild calculations, and in the most enthusiastic style—he raved, he shouted. The *contagion* soon became universal. All agreed he was right.

"A man coerced against his will
Is of the same opinion still."

The NERVOUS ATMOSPHERIC VIBRATIONS were too strong to be resisted—all were subjected by the nervous tempest. It is the same in *revival* Camp Meetings, Panics, and excitements.

MODERN SPIRITUALISM.

When the soft iron helix is rendered by induction magnetic, from the passage of the current round the coil of wire in which it is encircled, it has the capacity of raising and supporting a heavy weight. This force or power arises from the chemical action of the galvanic battery. Here is a silent, innocent, imperceptible cause producing astounding effects.

Only a few years have elapsed since the magnetic forces have been understood; now the laws of their action are admitted.

The magnetic current is so subtle and ethereal that it passes through a block of marble, granite, or glass as if these substances were not present. Yet when concentrated, it possesses the most wonderful power. It is one of the great forces of the earth, it plays a most important part in the economy of life.

If these remarks result in stimulating further investigation as to the mode of discharging the instrument of the will power, which knowledge has not been heretofore recognised, if we discover the means of accounting for the varied phenomena whose existence have been empirically known, and used to hold man, in his ignorance, the slave of bigotry and superstition, the author will have received ample reward for his effort in attempting to explain some of the "*mysteries*" appertaining to the "vital element."

APPENDIX.

The chronological history of the employment of anæsthetics in modern times may be recapitulated as follows :—

Sir *Humphry Davy's* declaration with regard to nitrous oxide gas : *Amongst its other properties it has that of destroying physical pain.* Davy did *not* convey the idea, or expound the principle, that the inhalation of narcotic and stimulating vapours would *destroy pain*, but confined his remarks to the nitrous oxide; nor did he imagine the production of a state of unconsciousness. Sir H. Davy, April 11th, 1799.

Anæsthetic state produced by vital magnetism, or nervous fluid. Removal of the entire breast for cancer. Dr. Jules Cloquet, Paris, April 12th, 1829.

Anæsthetic state induced by the inhalation of alcoholic fumes. Reduction of hip-joint. Dr. Collyer, Louisiana, Dec. 1839.

Anæsthetic state induced by Dr. Collyer on a child twenty-two months old. Entire removal of the globe of the eye for fungus hæmatodes. Dr. Rich, Bangor, Maine, Dec 1841.

Anæsthetic state induced by the inhalation of narcotic and stimulating vapours. Extraction of a tooth from Miss Allen. Dr. Collyer, Philadelphia, April, 1843.

Publication of the "Psychography," wherein at pages 26, 27, 28, 30, 32, 35, and 36, the inhalation of narcotic and stimulating vapours is stated to produce the unconscious or anæsthetic state. Author (Dr. Collyer), Philadelphia, May, 1843.

Report of lectures (vide *Lancet*) in *Liverpool Mail* and *Standard*. Dr. Collyer, Liverpool, Oct. 1843.

Protoxide of nitrogen. Extraction of tooth. Horace Wells, Hartford, Dec. 1844.

Publication in *Boston Medical and Surgical Journal* of the administration of opium and ether. Dr. E. R. Smilie, Boston, June, 1846.

Inhalation of sulphuric ether. Wm. T. G. Morton, Boston, Sept. 30th, 1846.

Experiments with chloroform on animals. Flourens, Paris, March, 1847.

Anæsthesia produced by chloric ether. Sir William Lawrence, London, June, 1847.

Anæ-thesia produced by the inhalation of chloroform. Dr. James Simpson, Edinburgh, Nov. 1847.

Anæsthesia by amylene. Dr. John Snow, London, June, 1857.

Bichloride of methylene. Dr. Benj. W. Richardson, London, June, 1867.

APPENDIX. 113

Report of the Committee on Animal Magnetism.

At a large and respectable meeting of the citizens of Boston, held at the Masonic Temple on the evening of the 22nd of June, 1841, Drs. Abner Phelps, Winslow Lewis, jun., and Francis Dana, were appointed a committee to select twenty-four gentlemen of the three learned professions in this city, for the purpose of investigating the claims of *Animal Magnetism,* as exhibited by Dr. Collyer.

The following gentlemen having been requested to attend to that duty, signified their acceptance of the appointment, and subsequently met at the Temple :— Rev. Messrs. Stowe, Gannett, Greenwood, Muzzy, Adams, Chapin, Neale, Turnbull, and Jones; Messrs. James, Power, Williams, Denny, Tolman, Peabody, and Plimpton, Barristers; Drs. Storer, Lane, Morrill, Flint, Dana, Strong, Ingalls, Lewis, and Stedman.

This committee associated with them several gentlemen, among whom were Drs. Adams and Stone, who attended some of the sittings.

Friday, 10 A.M., June 25th, 1841.

The committee organized by choosing Dr. William Ingalls Chairman, and Dr. Francis Dana, Secretary.

Dr. Collyer performed the customary manipulations upon his boy "Frederick," which were followed by the usual appearances. Many attempts were made by members of the committee to arouse him—such as stretching him upon the floor and firing two large pistols near his head—but without eliciting any symptoms of consciousness, unless it were in a spasm in the arm (tetanus), the like of which had been occurring for more than a quarter of an hour previous, and which happened at one of the discharges.

At this time a lad was introduced, who was suffering under the affection called chorea, or St. Vitus's dance. In answer to inquiries if any one knew him, the Rev. Mr. Stowe said he was a member of his church, and had been for several years, and was very exemplary ; and moreover, that he knew there could be no collusion between him and Dr. C. Dr. C. having performed the passes upon him for about fifteen minutes, there was a general quiet of the whole system, which before was continually writhed with involuntary twitchings and convulsions.

It is worthy of note, that while this process was going on, the first subject, still "asleep," was thrown into *strong spasms,* which continued during the remainder of his sleep. The Rev. Mr. Gannett asked Dr. C. if he intended to transfer those symptoms (of chorea) from the affected lad to the first subject. Dr. C. replied that he had no such intention, and moreover, that he was as much surprised as any one present at the circumstance. To the question put by the President, "Is the boy in an unnatural state ?" Dr. Stedman replied, "He appears to be in an unnatural state. Those spasms, I think, COULD NOT be feigned."

The committee adjourned, to meet again on Saturday at ten o'clock A.M.

I

Saturday, June 26th, 1841.

The committee met pursuant to adjournment, but without attending to any experiments, adjourned to Monday at ten o'clock A.M.

Monday, June 28th.

The committee met according to adjournment. A letter from the Hon. Judge Thacher was read. Dr. C. operated first upon his own subjects, with more or less of apparent success. It was then suggested by a member that it might be more satisfactory to the committee to have some subject not known by Dr. C., but with whom the committee were better acquainted: and that there was a gentleman present who was willing to subject himself to the process, and who was believed to be susceptible. Dr. C. consented to make an attempt. The gentleman alluded to was then presented. Several medical gentlemen of the committee, and some who were the strongest disbelievers of Animal Magnetism, expressed their high commendation of the character of the new subject for unimpeachable integrity and high attainments as a physician and a scholar, and said they knew he would enter into no scheme for misleading this audience or any other. Dr. C. then performed his usual process for about ten minutes, when the patient had gradually fallen asleep. Then as Dr. C. pointed his hand towards the face of the patient, he very suddenly with a shaking of the head and shoulders awoke: and half smiling, seemed partially self-possessed, and continued so for about ten seconds; but Dr. C. looking sternly at him, he reclined his head, and in about ten seconds more appeared asleep again. In a few seconds he awoke as before. He was again asleep under C.'s eye in a few seconds—then waking and beginning to explain how he felt, he put his hands upon the arms of his chair to rise, as if he bona fide thought he was now at liberty to leave, and rose half-way up; when (Dr. C. looking him sternly in the face) he fell back again into the chair, as if too weak to rise. He then rose to a perpendicular posture on his feet, and under the same circumstances and appearances sank again into his chair. Presently he rose again upon his feet, and turned towards the committee, and seeming to believe he was now at liberty, and not perceiving Dr. C., who stood close behind him with face and eyes sternly bent upon him, attempted again, with seeming eagerness, to explain how he felt; but he faltered every two or three words, pressing his hand hard against his eyes two or three times as though partially faint, and breaking off in the middle of a sentence without finishing any intelligible explanation, and having his hand again pressed over his eyes, rubbing them as though but partially awakened from deep sleep, he turned to take his seat, when he discovered that Dr. C. was close behind him and intent upon him. He then passed a distance of about three steps (Dr. C. now for the first time leaving him), and spoke connectedly and with an easy freedom. He said he felt a pleasant thrill in his arms and hands. "I did not lose my consciousness entirely, but felt confused, as you see I am. I attempted twice to speak while under the power of Dr. C., but could not." He says he never has spoken to Dr. C. but once, which was casually yesterday at the Natural History room, nor seen him more than twice, or ever communicated with him upon this subject. [He subsequently declined a request of the committee to submit himself again to experiment.]

The father of young Mr. Beals, a respectable merchant in this city, is present, and says he has not before seen his son so quiet for *seven years*, as he has been since operated upon by Dr. C.

The committee adjourned to half-past ten A.M. to-morrow.

Tuesday, June 29th.

The committee met pursuant to adjournment. Voted, to choose a sub-committee of five to examine the subject before and after being put into the so-called magnetic state. And Drs. Storer, Lewis, Morrell, J. H. Lane, and J. W. James, Esq., were chosen accordingly. The boy Frederick was examined by the sub-committee, who found nothing remarkable. Dr. C. commenced at twenty-two minutes before twelve, the boy declaring under the process, that he would not be put to sleep by Dr. C., because he had magnetized Mr. Beals. In about seven minutes there are strong twitchings of the muscles over the whole body, similar in appearance to those of the lad with chorea, who is present, and affirms that he has not felt any twitchings since Dr. C. began this time to magnetize Frederick, but prior to this had felt them, though comparatively slight since being magnetized by Dr. C. This present cessation of his tetanus was thought worth noting, though the magnetizing of Frederick, or his having the convulsions at this time, might have nothing to do with it. The Rev. Mr. Turnbull explained it by saying that the present quiet of Mr. Beal's muscles might be produced by his close attention to the prseent operation on Frederick ; and the Rev. Mr. T. asked Mr. B. if he felt calm when listening to his pastor (the Rev. Mr. Stowe) and being much interested ? He replied that he was more excited. The sub-committee was requested to give an opinion in regard to the muscular twitchings of Frederick, which had continued a long time. Dr. Storer stated his opinion that they might be feigned ; asked to say whether he thought they *were* feigned, he says—"I should choose not to be driven to an answer, but if you insist, I give it as my opinion that they *are* feigned." Dr. Morrell expressed his concurrence. Dr. Lane was not prepared to give an opinion. Mr. James doubted if they could be feigned. [Dr. Lewis out.] Dr. C. offered to have the boy left in that position (apparently an uncomfortable one), with gentlemen to watch him by turns for two, three, or four days, *to see* whether this state was feigned.

Mr. Stone, Student of Medicine from Salem, was introduced to the committee by Dr. Storer, who vouched for his good character, and that there could be no collusion between him and Dr. C., and added, "If he shall say Dr. C. puts him to sleep, I will believe it." Dr. C. made a trial. The only effect produced (at this time) was a heaviness of the arms, as if from great fatigue, and a strong contraction of the little finger, which he tried to overcome but said he could not.

Dr. C. had said to some members that Frederick was now in an unusually fine state for clairvoyance, when John C. Park, Esq., whom Dr. C. had declared to have the requisite continuity of thought, was put in communication with the lad. Mr. Park, without giving any intimation of his intended course, and avoiding all leading questions, asked the boy as to what he saw. The first two or three answers not being satisfactory to Mr. P., he willed him back again, he said, to where we were sitting, and then proceeded again. Each succeeding answer, as Mr. P. declares, was correctly descriptive of the same things, in the same order, and at the same times that Mr. P. had the ideas of them in his mind directing attention to them.

Mr. Park's Question.—1. What do you see?
Frederick's Answer.—Something high.
Mr. Park's statement made on each answer after the conclusion of the whole experiments.—The building west side of Bowdoin Square.
Mr. P.—2. What colour is it?
Ans.—Black or white—not very black.
Mr. P.'s statement.—It is of granite.
Mr. P.—3. What is there about it? are there any streets?
Ans.—One on each side.
Mr. P.'s statement.—Such is the fact.
Mr. P.—4. What do you see now?
Ans.—A door.
Mr. P.'s statement.—I viewed in imagination the door of the gaol in Levere Street.
Mr. P.—5. Anything about it?
Ans.—Only the steps there.
Mr. P.'s statement.—There are steps to it.
Mr. P.—6. Now pass into that door with me through an entry, and what do you see?
Ans.—Oh! a great many doors.
Mr. P.'s statement.—I was in imagination at this time, and during the two following questions, in a hall of the gaol, having in it nine doors all in view.
Mr. P.—7. How many? Count them.
Ans.—1, 2, 3—I can't count them.
Mr. P.—8. Yes, you can—I can, and so can you. Try again.
Ans.—1, 2, 3, 4, 5, 6, 7—oh! there's more than that; I can't count them. It's a cold place—I don't want to stay here.
Mr. P.—9. Well then, we'll leave this place and go to another. What do you see?
Ans.—A door.
Mr. P.'s statement.—I contemplated the door of Williamson's cell.
Mr. P.—10. Well, we'll go into that door.
Ans.—Oh, we can't, it's all barred up. We can't go in.
Mr. P.'s statement.—It is kept bolted of course.
Mr. P.—11. Why not? Yes we can. We will go in. Are we in.
Ans.—Yes.
Mr. P.—12. What do you see there?
Ans.—A man.
Mr. P.—13. Anybody else there?

APPENDIX. 117

Ans.—No; one man and no more.
Mr. P.'s statement.—Williamson alone is kept there.
Mr. P.—14. What is he doing?
Ans.—Sitting there.
Mr. P.—15. What does he sit on?
Ans.—Something dirty.
Mr. P.'s statement.—Their beds are dirty.
Mr. P.—16. Do you see anything else?
Ans.—Only the black thing over there.
Mr. P.'s statement.—I knew not what the boy meant at the time, but went directly to the gaol, and Williamson had a black article up against the wall to lean against as he sat.
Mr. P.—17. Now we'll turn round, and what do you see?
Ans.—A small white thing, round.
Mr. P.'s statement.—A tub, for necessary purposes, which is round.
Mr. P.—18. What is it for?
Ans.—It's nasty—I don't want to tell. [Exhibiting great disgust.]
Mr. P.'s statement.—Correctly described thus.
Mr. P.—19. Well, you've told enough about that. What do you see now?
Ans.—A window.
Mr. P.'s statement.—I was directing attention to the window.
Mr. P.—20. Look out at that window.
Ans.—I can't.
Mr. P.—21. Why?
Ans.—It's dirty.
Mr. P.'s statement.—I was wishing to have him speak of the iron grates to it, but do not comprehend his answer.

Mr. P. then said—Now we'll go to another part. What do you see? But the answers to this and other questions not being satisfactory, Mr. P. said, Well, I don't know where you are. You are where I'm not, and proceeded no further.

The following is Mr. Park's certificate on the above:—

"I hereby certify that the expressions above attributed to me, are in substance correct. ."JOHN C. PARK."

Adjourned to half-past ten o'clock, Thursday, A.M.

Thursday, July 1st.

The committee met pursuant to adjournment.

Voted, That Dr. Gregerson (he being present) be requested to state his late experience upon the subject of the committee's inquiries. Dr. G. rose and gave a very interesting account in detail of the manner of his late conviction of the reality of some of the phenomena asserted by the advocates of Animal Magnetism. He says he began two or three evenings since, while entirely faithless upon this subject, to manipulate upon a gentleman happening to be with him, who was so far a sceptic as to have said shortly before that he wished Dr. C. would try to magnetize him before his evening audience, and he would feign sleep until Dr. C. announced that he was in the magnetic condition, and then break out in laughter. Presently the subject appeared asleep. When he was shortly after awake again, he was accused by Dr. G. of doing to him as he had said he would to Dr. Collyer—*i.e.*, feigning sleep. But he (the subject) declared he had *not been* asleep. Yet when questioned, it appeared that he was utterly ignorant of a remarkable noise that had occurred in the meantime, as also of Dr. G.'s going to shut the door. Since this first time, Dr. G. thinks he has several times put him asleep most unequivocally, and elicited somnambulic phenomena. [The committee had the opportunity of witnessing this by Dr. Gregerson, in the lower room of the Temple, July 6th.]

Dr. Dana, the Secretary, being unwell, S. F. Plimpton was chosen Secretary, *pro tem.*

An unsuccessful attempt was made to magnetize a new subject.

At 12 o'clock Dr. C. commences operating upon Mr. Stone, before mentioned, in whom gentlemen had expressed their confidence. At about twelve minutes past 12 o'clock he stands up, and Dr. C. continues his "willing" for a minute or two longer. Then Dr. C. ceasing and stepping aside, Mr. Stone is asked to state how he had felt, &c. But he stood as he was, mute and motionless, for more than half a minute, as though he heeded nothing that was said or done, and with his eyes still fixed as they had been. He is asked, "Can't you speak?" He soon faintly replies, "Yes, sir," but still continues with his eyes and body fixed as before, and in about ten seconds says, "I do feel very peculiarly indeed," still without having stirred eye or limb. In about one minute more he seemed more self-possessed, and began the following narration :—

"I had a sort of confused feeling, which I have not recovered from even "now. When I was put the question how I felt, I thought I would answer, "and tried to do so, but felt somehow not disposed for it. I felt a peculiar "sensation in my whole body, in my arms and legs, and do so even now ; and "when Dr. C. stepped off from me, leaving me to myself, I felt I could stand "there comfortable for a considerable length of time, and had to make a strong "effort to move. When you first asked me to speak, I felt you were waiting "for me all around, and yet I could not speak."

At thirty-two minutes past twelve, Rev. Mr. Jones begins to operate on Frederick, and at thirty-seven minutes past twelve he appears asleep. Mr. Jones asked him various questions, as to what he (Mr. J.) had on his head at the times the questions were put; and most of the answers were correct, and so with regard to several other things, Dr. C. being kept some distance off.

The Rev. Mr. Turnbull moved that the labours of the committee be now concluded, but after some discussion, the vote thereon was nearly unanimous against it.

The committee adjourned to 3 o'clock P.M. of Tuesday next.

Tuesday, July 6th.

The committee met according to adjournment.

Dr. C. relates that Mr. Stone, Student of the Medical School to which Dr. Storer lectures, and in whom gentlemen had expressed their confidence, had told him that he (Mr. Stone) had magnetized one of his friends, Mr. —— ;

APPENDIX. 119

and Dr. C. adds, that he himself, on introduction, has done the same—all of which Mr. Stone, being present, confirms.

While in default of a subject, and there was no other present business before the committee, considerable debate arose on the question of Dr. Gregerson, stating the experience he had had since the last meeting. It was voted that he be requested to state it. Dr. G. acknowledged he had had some new experience, but declined stating it because the vote was not unanimous. A few had voted in the negative, saying that the character of Dr. Gregerson was such as might give his statements more weight with this committee than they should have.

Mr. ——, the friend before mentioned of Mr. Stone, is brought in, and submits to the operation, only on the condition expressed in the following vote, viz.:—

Voted, That the name of no new subject be mentioned out of this hall.

Voted, That the sub-committee, appointed June 29th, officiate during the experiment on Mr. ——; and in the absence of Dr. Lane, Dr. Adams be substituted.

Dr. Storer and others, who are still sceptics, express themselves as entirely satisfied of the conscientious and veracious character of Mr. ——, and that there is no collusion between him and Dr. C. Age 26.

The sub-committee report a soft pulse in the patient at 96 per minute—skin moist—hands rather cold and moist. Dr. C.'s pulse at 96. He commences the operation at twenty minutes before five. At thirteen minutes before five, the patient having appeared asleep for a few minutes, Dr. C. applies his hand abov the patient's, as if to attract it upward—when directly the fingers of the sleeper begin to twitch and tremble, and presently his whole hand to tremble or vibrate through the space of at least an inch. Dr. C. now applies his above the patient's other hand, and then that too twitches and trembles in like manner. In the same manner Dr. C. applies a common horse-shoe magnet, and with the same effect. Dr. C. says the patient is now in a semi-state. At two minutes before five o'clock, Dr. C. performs a few more passes, and asks, "Mr. ——, do you see me?" to which Mr. —— answers, "Yes." "Any one else?" Answer, "No." To calls first imitating those of Dr. C., and then very loud calls of Mr. —— made at his ears, by Dr. Storer, Dr. Morrell, Dr. Adams, and others, he returns no answer. Dr. C. then says more gently, "Did you hear any noise, Mr. ——?" He answers, "No." A loud noise was here made, and Dr. C. asks, "Did you hear any noise then?" Answer, "No." Other loud and very loud noises were then made, and after each of them the same question was put by Dr. C., and the same answer given. The patient's eyes were opened. Dr. Storer reports that "the eyeball seems uncontrolled, and to have an involuntary vibrating or rolling motion." The patient's pulse is reported at ninety-six, the same as before. Endeavours to tickle the nose, ears, ribs, and other sensitive parts, fail entirely; while his brother, now present, states that "compared with other persons he is very easily tickled indeed." Dr. C. procures several answers from him in a "mental" journey to the Tremont House. Then being asked by Dr. C. "in which room are we?" he says, "In the bar." Further questioned, he says, "There are three persons in the bar." A most trustworthy gentleman, hitherto a sceptic, goes as quickly as possible to the spot and finds three persons there, who had been there, they assured him, for more than fifteen minutes, and that no other person had been about there in the meantime. In a somnambulic journey to the lower room in the Temple, being questioned by Dr. C. as to how many persons there are there, he says, "Five." In fact there were four—but Dr. C. asks, "Did you count yourself?" and he answers, "Yes." Dr. C. puts the following by request : "What has one of them in his hand ?" He replies, "—— foot." It is reported that the thing held up was in fact a chair, and that it was held by the foot of it. Dr. C. now asked the patient what foot it was he meant, and he said, "of a stool."

At fourteen minutes before six, Dr. C. commences the upward passes to awake the patient. At twelve minutes before six he begins gradually to move his head, and at ten minutes before six has it erect against the chair, sighs deeply, shrugs the shoulders, and presses the hands against his face and eyes, rubbing the latter, and stretching as if just waked from a deep sleep. Thus his sleeping lasted for an hour and ten minutes, during all which time every part of him, unless moved by persons present, was perfectly composed as in sleep, except so far as was necessary to perform the acts above described, and except that a clapping of hands at his ear produced a motion of the head, and did the same on repetition.

Mr. ——, gradually recovering himself, begins to remark that his arms were quite stiff and sore from rowing yesterday, when he came here, so that he could not bend them, but are now limber and free from soreness, and his back, which was quite stiff and sore when he came here, has now but little of soreness. Asked by the Rev. Dr. Greenwood—"How long do you think you have been asleep?" He says, "About ten minutes"—"I recollect I saw Dr. Collyer and no one else." [Dr. C. says this must have been when he was in the semi-state.] "I feel just as if waked from a natural sleep—I felt no one handle or touch me during my sleep, nor recollect any visions or dreams, or of hearing any noises." The Rev. Mr. Gannett says to him, "You pressed your chest and crossed your arms against your breast when waking, as though pained. Did you feel any pain during the last four or five minutes?" He replies, "Not at all." He says he tried not to go to sleep, and thought of everything he could to keep awake. Never saw any magnetizing till he saw it lately here by Dr. Collyer, and that he always calls the leg of a chair the foot of it.

Voted, That each of the sub-committee be requested to state his opinion upon the facts observed.

Dr. Storer—"I was hitherto entirely sceptical, and consider this last as the only satisfactory experiment I have seen. I have now no doubt that Mr. —— was in an unnatural state."

Dr. Lewis—"I have had no doubts of the other subjects having been in the unnatural state, and of course, have none that this was so."

Dr. Morrell states substantially the same as Dr. Storer.

Dr. Adams—"I feel obliged to say, I think the patient was in a very strange and unnatural state of nerve."

J. W. James, Esq., concurs generally in the foregoing statements.

Mr. Stone says, "I do not hesitate to say, I think Mr. —— was in an unnatural state, having seen him so twice before, producing it once myself, and having known him intimately as a room-mate."

Dr. Storer, in reply to a question, says that he now has no doubt that this unnatural state was produced by Dr. Collyer. "I have before been a sceptic, but am now free to say I am so no longer."

The foregoing record of this meeting was then read, and sanctioned by all concerned. On the motion of Dr. Storer,

Voted, That the unanimous thanks of this committee be presented to the gentleman who has submitted himself to the operations of Dr. Collyer this afternoon.

The committee having ascertained from Dr. Collyer that *he* would expect some public expression from them, after having convinced them at the expense of so much trouble; and after remarks by the Rev. Mr. Gannett, Dr. Greenwood, and A. Peabody, Esq., it was deemed proper to give it, and,

After considerable discussion, in which Rev. Messrs. Greenwood, Gannett, Turnbull, Jones, Muzzy, and Chapin, Drs. Storer, Adam, and Flint, and Messrs. Peabody, James, and others took part, the following resolution was adopted unanimously, with a view to its publication—viz.:

Resolved, That while this committee refrain from expressing any decisive opinion as to the science or principle of Animal Magnetism, they freely confess that, in the experiments of Dr. Collyer, certain appearances have been presented which cannot be explained on the supposition of collusion, or by a reference to any physiological principles known to them.

After providing for the publication of this record, the meeting dissolved.

WILLIAM INGALLS, *Chairman*.
S. F. PLIMPTON, *Secretary, pro tem.*

It may perhaps be a satisfaction to some, who respect logical exactness more than random raillery, to examine the following calculation on the doctrine of chances, showing the great improbability of Frederick's GUESSING correct answers to Mr. Park's questions, as given in the above report. We shall refer to them by their numbers as above given. It will be seen that we omit in our calculation many of the correct answers, just as if in those cases there were no other thing which his mind could be led to fix on for his guess, and therefore it were no guess at all. This, however, is far from true, and it makes a very large concession:—

1. In relation to the *third* answer, suppose (to be within bounds) that only one in four of the buildings in the city has a street on each side of it; and the chances of giving this answer with correctness, in a mere guess, are seen to be one in four, and the ratio of probability is 1-4.

2. On the eighth answer: in what proportion, let it be asked, of all the places within doors can he be seen at once seven and more doors—*i.e.*, as many as eight? Probably not one in fifty. Let then the ratio be 1-50.

3. On the tenth answer: suppose that, of all the inner doors in the city, one-twentieth of them are thus barred up at mid-day, and the chances

of guessing such a description as the boy did, with correctness, would be only one in twenty ; and the ratio of probability in guessing thus, 1-20.

4. On the thirteenth answer : suppose that of all the apartments in the city, the proportion which have in them, between one and two o'clock P.M., just one person and not more, and that person a man, and not a woman or child, is (we will say, to be within bounds) one in five; and the ratio of probability for one's guessing thus rightly would be 1-5.

5. On the fourteenth answer : suppose that of all the articles that would be likely to attract attention in all the apartments of the city, not more than one in three could be called round, and the ratio of probability is 1-3.

6. On the eighteenth answer : it may be safely said that of the articles in our apartments, not more than one in five could well be thus described in such severe Saxon, and the ratio of probability is 1-5.

7. On the nineteenth: suppose other visible articles in apartments will average as numerous as windows, and then the chances of guessing a window with correctness will be one in two, and the ratio 1-2.

Now multiply all these ratios together—(according to Edin. Encyc., Art. Chances, or Hedge's Logic)

$$\tfrac{1}{4} \times \tfrac{1}{50} \times \tfrac{1}{20} \times \tfrac{1}{5} \times \tfrac{1}{3} \times \tfrac{1}{5} \times \tfrac{1}{2} = \tfrac{1}{600,000},$$

and the chances of *guessing* correctly in all these instances taken together prove to be only one in more than half a million. Towards making up this number, each of the supposed failures counts only one by way of offset.

We think the estimate we have given of the probabilities in the instances we have selected above is far less than they would bear, to say nothing of the correct answers we have omitted. But unless one can gainsay this estimate as too large, he must admit (600,000 to 1) either that one of our citizens, whom w are accustomed to trust, is duping the public on an extensive and difficult plan, or else that there is something in clairvoyance.

This is not the only case of this kind in which, in order to disprove clairvoyance, it will be necessary to implicate, to a similar certainty—*i.e.*, many thousands to one—the veracity of some of our most respectable citizens. We think therefore the argument grows serious, to say the least.

The twenty-six gentlemen who composed this committee were amongst the most eminent in their respective professions in the United States. No one can therefore but treat such a document with the respect it so justly merits. All were desirous of arriving at the truth. The unanimous decision of less than half the number would consign a human being to death in a trial of murder. It is therefore exceedingly curious that the verdict of twenty-six of the most intelligent men in Boston, U.S., should not be received as conclusive evidence. "There are more things in heaven and earth, Horatio, than are dreamt of in your philosophy."

From " Galignani's Messenger," Paris, Feb. 18th, 1847.

" M. Serres communicated to the Academy the details of several experiments " with ether on rabbits, but as they add little, except in the way of confirmation,

APPENDIX.

" to what was stated in the last sitting by M. Gruby, we do not think it neces-
" sary to give them here. In direct connexion with this subject, however, we
" lay before our readers the following letter, which we have received from Mr.
" Wells, the first discoverer of the scientific application of intoxication as the
" means of rendering the body insensible to pain. We regret that, at a
" moment when the question of the value of this discovery, and the extent to
" which it may be safely carried, is under discussion in the Academy of Sciences,
" Mr. Wells has not made a communication to that body. The facts stat
" by Mr. Wells are highly important, and are entitled to the more considera-
" tion as coming from such a source. He says :—'As you have recentl
" published an extract from the *Boston Medical and Surgical Journal*, which
" recognises me as the discoverer of the happy effects produced by the inhala-
" tion of exhilarating gas or vapour in the performance of surgical operations,
" I will now offer some suggestions in reference to this subject. Reasoning
" from analogy, I was led to believe that surgical operations might be performed
" without pain, by the fact that an individual when much excited from ordinary
" causes, may receive severe wounds without manifesting the least pain ; as, for
" instance, the man who is engaged in combat may have a limb severed from
" his body, after which he testifies that it was attended with no pain at the
" time ; and so the man who is intoxicated with spirituous liquor may
" be treated severely without his manifesting pain, as the frame seems in this
" state to be more tenacious of life than under ordinary circumstances. By these
" facts, I was led to inquire if the same result would not follow by the inhala-
" tion of some exhilarating gas, the effects of which would pass off immediately,
" leaving the system none the worse for its use. I accordingly procured some
" nitrous oxide gas, resolving to make the first experiment on myself by having
" a tooth extracted, which was done without any painful sensations. I then
" performed the same operation on twelve or fifteen others, with the like results ;
" this was in November, 1844 ; being a resident of Hartford, Con. (U.S.), I
" proceeded to Boston the following month (December), in order to present my
" discovery to the Medical Faculty—first making it known to Drs. Warren,
" Hayward, Jackson, and Morton, the two last of whom subsequently pub-
" lished the same, without mention of our conference. Since this discovery was
" first made, I have administered nitrous oxide gas and the vapour of ether to
" about fifty patients, my operations having been limited to this small number
" in consequence of a *protracted* illness which immediately ensued on my return
" home from Boston, in January, 1845. Much depends on the state of
" mind of the patient during the inhalation of gas or vapour. If the individual
" takes it with the determination to submit to a surgical operation, he has
" no disposition to exert the muscular system ; whereas, under other circum-
" stances, it seems impossible to restrain him from over-exertion ; he becomes
" perfectly uncontrollable. It is well to instruct all patients of this fact before
" the inhalation takes place. The temperament and physical condition of the
" patient should be well marked before administering *the vapour of ether;*
" persons whose lungs are much affected, should not be permitted to inhale
" this vapour, as serious injuries have resulted from it in such cases. Nitrous
" oxide gas, or protoxide of nitrogen, is much less liable to do injury, and is

"more agreeable to inhale, producing at the same time equal insensibility to
"all painful sensations. It may be taken without the least inconvenience by
"those who become choked almost *to strangulation with ether;* in fact, I have
"never seen or heard of a single instance where this gas has proved in the
"least detrimental. *This discovery does not consist in the use of any one speci-*
"*fied gas or vapour: for anything which causes a certain degree of nervous*
"*excitement, is all that is requisite to produce insensibility to pain.* Conse-
"quently, the only question to be settled is, which exhilarating agent is least
"likely to injure the system? The less atmospheric air admitted into the lungs
"with any gas or vapour, the better, the more satisfactory will be the result of
"the operation. Those who have been accustomed to use much intoxicating
"beverage, cannot be easily affected in this manner. With cases of dislocated
"joints, the exhilarating gas operates like a charm; all the muscles become
"relaxed, and but a very little effort will serve to replace the limb in its socket,
"and while the operation is being performed, the muscles do not contract
"as when in the natural state, but are as easily managed as those of a
"corpse. Allow me to add that, as I have had no opportunity of reading
"any of the French professional reports or discussions on this subject, I
"shall remain in Paris until the 27th inst., and in the interval I should be
"pleased to impart such information as I may have acquired by a close
"observation of the various phenomena connected with this interesting
"subject.

"'HORACE WELLS.

"'Rue d'Alger, Feb. 1847.'"

The necessity of republishing this letter entire, arises from the fact that at the time it was written, as will be observed, *all the documents* were then in my possession, proving the surgical operations in 1839, 1842, and 1843 during the anæsthetic state, "induced by the inhalation of narcotic and stimulating vapours."

The Hon. Truman Smith says:—"Mr. Wells attended a lecture by Mr. "G. Q. Culton on the 10th of December, 1844. A Mr. Cooley having inhaled "the gas, and becoming much excited, contused his ankles without experiencing "pain. Wells had the gas administered to himself next day, and a tooth ex- "tracted."

There *was no reasoning by analogy.* The whole experiment was the result of an impulsive idea, which *he abandoned* entirely after a few trials in the following *month.* It has been shown elsewhere, that Mr. Wells had no philosophy on the subject; he never dreamt of producing a state of unconscious insensibility.

I also published in the *Morning Chronicle, Medical Times,* and *Critic* the history of my discovery. The following appeared in the *Critic* of April 10th, 1847, No. 119:—

" *To the Editor of ' The Critic.'*

"SIR,—My attention has just been called to a statement of Dr. Wells, as given "in No. 114 (March 6th) of the *Critic,* relative to his priority in the discovery

APPENDIX. 125

"of the effects of *ether* in *producing insensibility* to physical pain. I have
" therefore the pleasure to forward you a counter-statement, of my own claims,
" in addition to that which you did me the honour to publish in your valuable
" Journal of Mental Philosophy. (See *Critic*, No. 106, for January 9th, 1847.)
" Dr. Wells, of Hartford, Connecticut, states that he performed the experiments
" *in November*, 1844, and that he, in the following month (December), CALLED
" on Drs. Warren, Hayward, Jackson, and Morton, and made known *his* dis-
" covery. But *he complains*, that Drs. Morton and Jackson subsequently
" published the discovery, without mention of this conference *with* him! Time,
" indeed, sets all things even; men may attempt to overreach their fellows, in
" consequence of a supposed superiority of position, but it only requires a
" steady adherence to truth, combined with energy, in order to expose the
" upstart pretenders, and secure merit its just claims. I have been a public
" lecturer on *Physiology* now eight years, and have written on the particular
" subject now claiming public attention—namely, the inhalation of "*Stimulating*
" *and Narcotic Vapours*," in order to produce *nervous congestion* of the brain,
" so that surgical operations could be performed without pain to the patient.
" Had I not been prevented in consequence of illness, I would have long since
" VISITED LONDON WITH MY PUBLICATIONS,* which prove my discovery and appli-
" cation of the same in the early part of the year 1843, two years before Dr.Wells
" called on Drs. Morton and Jackson! I extract the following lecture from
" the *Providence Evening Chronicle* (U.S.) of March 17th, 1843. To the
" English reader it must be stated that Providence is situated within a few
" miles of Hartford, Dr. Wells's residence, also only forty from Boston, the
" residence of Drs. Morton and Jackson. I also, in Boston, delivered more
" than twenty lectures on this very topic in 1842 and 1843. The following is
" the lecture:—
      " 'The lecture of Dr. Collyer, at Westminster Hall, last evening, was on the
" Philosophy of the Nervous Force. Man must be called an electrical machine
" —indeed he was so, most truly; he was governed by its laws, and exhibited
" most of the phenomena connected with that fluid. Magnetic sleep was a
" congestion of the brain produced by the transmission of the nervous force
" from one person to another. To illustrate this in brain fever, where there is
" an over-action of that part of the body, we find the patient has cold hands
" and feet; here is a withdrawal from those parts of the nervous force to supply
" this extra action of the brain. *He noticed the beautiful action of the lungs in
" this connexion.* Monotony would produce sleep on the most irritable when
" all opiates fail; waking was only the result of the constant stimulus of the
" variety which meet our gaze. Printers often experience this in a blurred
" sheet, or a double impression on the same sheet. By looking at any object
" for a long time a dimness would come over the eyes, languor, &c.; in fact, all
" the approaching attributes of sleep or a congestion of the brain, as in common
" sleep or the mesmeric sleep, would be produced. He further alluded to the
" action of the nervous force as connected with the brain. Men in strife

------

* Lost in Mexico and California in 1849 and 1851.

APPENDIX.

"receive bruises and wounds, and are not sensible of the fact at the time, in
"consequence of the great excitement of the brain, producing a deadness of the
"outer surface, or in other words, a withdrawal of the nervous force to supply
"the increased action of the central action portions of the brain. Any excitement
"would produce the same result; as we see in the Hindoo widow, in the Indian
"of the forest, who seems at times wholly indifferent to pain, and will bear the
"most excruciating torture without a murmur. In cases of religious excite-
"ment the same action is made manifest. Persons under this religious frenzy
"do what under ordinary circumstances they could not do, until at length the
"brain becomes exhausted, and the subject falls into a swoon, in which they lie
"for hours and even days. By exciting a person's vanity we have *the same*
"result; SURGICAL OPERATIONS have been performed, where the patient has
"borne the pain with the greatest fortitude when his feelings have been appealed
"to. A Roman general once boasted of the great power of the Romans to
"bear pain, and plunged his arm into the fire until it dropped off. In a con-
"dition where there is an equilibrium of the system, the sting of a mosquito
"will almost drive one mad. Dr. Collyer gave the statement of a celebrated
"French surgeon (Baron Larrey), who accompanied Napoleon in all his cam-
"paigns, to substantiate his position. This *surgeon stated that operations* were
"always better borne by the soldiers if performed immediately after an engage-
"ment, while *the excitement was on,* than if performed at a later period.'

"The next month I published a work, wherein at page 26 I use these words
"(after having performed the experiments publicly):—*The power to produce
"this congestive state of the nervous system is not confined to the nervo-vital fluid
"of a second person. The same state of things may be brought about by mental
"excitement, accompanied by muscular action;* THE INHALING OF NARCOTIC
"AND STIMULATING VAPOURS. I performed a variety of experiments in con-
"nexion with inhalation—demonstrating its power to produce congestion of the
"brain. I have also, at pages 26 and 27, given the Delphic oracle as an
"example in these words:—'A goatherd fed his flocks on the acclivity of Mount
"Parnassus. As the animals wandered here and there in pursuit of food, they
"happened to approach a deep and long chasm in the rock. From this chasm
"*a vapour issued,* and the goats had no *sooner inhaled a portion* of the vapour
"than they began to play and frisk about with singular agility. The goatherd
"observing this, and curious to discover the cause, *held his head over the chasm;
"in a short time the fumes* having ascended to *his brain,* he threw himself into
"a variety of strange attitudes, and uttered words which were supposed to
"have a prophetic meaning. A temple was erected on the spot, and dedicated
"to Apollo. The particular apartment of the oracle was *immediately* over the
"chasm from which the vapours issued. A priestess delivered the responses—
"she sat upon a tripod or three-legged stool, perforated with holes *over the seat
"of the vapours.* THE CONDITION of the priestess was IDENTICAL WITH THAT
"of the *mesmerized* PERSON.'

"Though I performed a great many minor operations during a condition
"induced by the inhaling of the stimulating vapours, I was at that time pre-
"judiced in favour of that induced by the nervo-vital fluid from a second person

APPENDIX. 127

"in the mesmeric state; during which condition I had seen a great many
"capital operations performed without pain to the patient.

"Again, at page 32, in explaining the feats of the Egyptian magicians, I use
"these words:—'The only difference between my experiments and those
"mentioned by Lane in his admirable work on Egypt is, that in my case, the
"boy's brain was rendered sentient to the mental *image* by the nervous agency
"from a second person; whereas the boys used by the Egyptian magi were
"caused to inhale narcotic fumes, PRODUCING IN BOTH INSTANCES THE IDEN-
"TICAL STATE OF BRAIN.'

"In Louisiana, in 1839, I reduced a dislocation of the hip-joint of a man, who
"was rendered insensible by the inhalation of vapour arising from rum. It is
"a very common practice among the negroes to inhale these fumes, and thereby
"produce total unconsciousness. It must be taken into consideration that my
"experiments were not performed in a corner, but before the world, and in the
"very city where Drs. Jackson and Morton reside, and that I have explicitly
"demonstrated that whenever the brain was the seat of special action, the ner-
"vous force was robbed from all parts of the body in order to meet the increased
"demand of the brain. The lungs are the manufacturing organs of the system
"—they supply the wasted powers—their function being particularly in action
"during sleep; whenever any stimulating vapour is applied to them, their pro-
"ductive function is much increased. This is the case in the inhalation of
"ether, alcohol, protoxide of nitrogen, or any other stimulating vapour. In
"1835 I was a student at the London University College. Dr. Turner, Pro-
"fessor of Chemistry, used to administer to those pupils of his class who chose
"to inhale it, the laughing or protoxide of nitrogen gas. On one occasion the gas
"gave out, and sulphuric ether was substituted. Mr. Belmain, Dr. Turner's
"assistant, will no doubt remember my having inhaled the ether, and how long
"I remained in the laboratory in an insensible state, and which will never be
"forgotten by me. Now is it likely that when engaged in the investigation of
"this subject in 1842, I purposely neglected the experience I had bought
"in 1835? In fine, I have shown clearly that Drs. Morton and Jackson got
"the idea from Dr. Wells, a gentleman I never heard of, but who must have
"heard of my experiments in *connexion with inhalation*, or as they were face-
"tiously called 'the bowl of molasses' experiments;' for there was no editor in
"the United States who had not a joke at my expense, in connexion with my
"experiments.

"I remain, most respectfully yours,
"ROBERT H. COLLYER, M.D.

"St. Helier's, Jersey, March 26th, 1847."

"Saltillo, September 22nd, 1849.

"Exmo. Señor Gobernador del Estados de Cohuhuila Roberto H. Collyer,
"Doctor en Medicena, tiene el honor de companacer ante V. E. accompanande
"el diploma que accredita la Facultad Medica de Cuidadamo. Jesus Maria Cam
"pos, Presidente del y Ayuntamento de Parras, con que manifiesto á V. E.
"habeo poseido otros dos titulos peso habien dosidac asaltado par unos

"ladrones (23) me fueron robador defau Da me Salum^te el que tengo el honor de
"acompania á V. E. Para que empuesto de su contenido se digne concedes me
"la licensia correspondentio par exercer mi facultad en Estados de Cohuhuila
"A. V. E. suplico se digne de exetar a conformidad.
 Seal.   "ROBERT H. COLLYER.

"Saltillo, Setiembre 23 de 1849.

"Visto y examinado el titulo que presenta el interisado.
                                            RODRIGUES, Gobierno.

To which are added the licence of the President of the Municipal Council of Saltillo.

It was in the Sierra Madre Mountains on the 31st of July, 1849, that I was "attacked by the banditti of twenty-three, who took from me my effects, together with the documents referred to in the letter to the *Critic* of April, 1847. The original of the Mexican official document is now in my possession.

The following from Dr. Henry Bennet, shows how Mr. Wells fulfilled his promise.

                                    "Mentone, October 31st, 1868.
"MY DEAR DR. COLLYER,

"I have no recollection of having received any further documents from Mr. 'Wells after the publication of my letter in the *Lancet* in 1847. Indeed I think "I may safely say that I did not again hear from him on that or any other "subject. I am not mistaken, his death occurred not long afterwards. Trust-"ing you will succeed in establishing your position, of which fact, however, I "do not doubt,
                    "Faithfully yours,
                                    "HENRY BENNET."

Ten months subsequent, Horace Wells committed suicide in New York.

It must be conclusive evidence, that had either Wells or Morton been engaged in the investigation of producing an anæsthetic state prior to their haphazard, accidental trials, their researches would have been made known. Not a scrap of the kind has ever been adduced. Mr. Morton was so ignorant of the chemical nature of sulphuric ether, that when he went to Dr. Charles Jackson he said, "*What kind of looking stuff is it?*" Dr. Jackson was most unlikely to suggest its use as a substitute for the protoxide of nitrous gas, he never dreamt that it would produce an anæsthetic state; in fine, we have his and Morton's conjoint affidavit to the effect that neither himself or Morton *knew or believed the same to have ever been known or used before.*

If we cannot believe Morton and Jackson under oath, when are they to be believed?

If any one will compare the extract of lectures published in the Boston, Philadelphia, and Providence newspapers in 1842 and 1843, with those published by Mr. Wells in *Galignani's Messenger* in February, 1847, he will see that the one is a copy of the other.

APPENDIX.

Lille, France, June 5th, 1870.

"My dear Doctor,—As to Dr. E. E. Marcy, on whose evidence the Hon.
"Truman Smith and others seem to place so much reliance, I have merely to
"extract verbatim what he wrote to *The New York Journal of Commerce*,
"December 30th, 1846, in order to show how completely ignorant he was at
"that time of the action of anæsthetics. He says, 'My opinion in regard to the
"use of nitrous oxide gas, sulphuric ether, or any other stimulant which acts
"upon the system in such a manner as to render the body insensible to external
"impressions, is that it is *decidedly unsafe*, and in no given case can we be
"certain that it will not cause *congestion of the brain* and lungs. I HAVE
"KNOWN the use of both the first named articles (nitrous oxide and sulphuric
"ether) to give rise to temporary *congestion of brain and insanity*.'
"These words of Dr. E. E. Marcy were written before the use of *anæsthetic agents
"had been demonstrated* universally by the profession, December, 1846. Many
"years subsequent, when their use was established, Dr. Marcy then *remembers
"for the first time* having *administered sulphuric ether* in October, 1844, and *two
"months before Wells's* experiment, *to some person*, and actually cut *an encysted
"tumour* of about the size of an English walnut. It was entirely successful.
"Dr. Marcy singularly forgets in 1858 what he said in 1846, and remembers
"in 1858 what he forgot in 1846. Is it probable that a person entertaining such
"extreme opinions as producing *congestion of brain and lungs resulting in
"insanity* in 1846, would have been the person to perform a *surgical operation*
"with entire success in 1844, similar to cutting out an encysted tumour of the
"size of a *Yankee nutmeg*, and that no mention should have been made of so
"wonderful an exploit at the time, nor even in the famous letter of 1846 ?

"No newspaper, no medical journal, is communicated with at the time, yet we
"find Dr. E. E. Marcy in 1846 and 1847 and subsequent years, most ready to
"appear in print in order to destroy the claims of Wm. T. G. Morton, of Boston.
"Yet this gifted individual, who in the most *decided* and unqualified manner
"declares that nitrous oxide and sulphuric ether are 'decidedly unsafe, pro-
"ducing congestion of the brain, lungs, and insanity,' in 1846 has the temerity
"to cut out tumours of the size of English walnuts in 1844 with *entire success*,
"and that too with the aid of sulphuric ether.

"Really, that such wild, unfounded misrepresentations should be credited by
"a man of the intelligence of the Hon. Truman Smith is truly astonishing. Yet
"this is the kind of material which he uses to vindicate the claims of the few
"haphazard, accidental experiments performed by Horace Wells in December,
"1844, and January, 1845, which he *abandoned* as being convinced that *they
"had no practical value. Vide* Reports before Committee of Congress. I would
"not have taken the trouble to expose this inconsistency, had not the late
"distinguished Sir James Simpson referred to it in his last publication.

"Yours very truly,

"ROBERT H. COLLYER.

"To Dr. Benjamin W. Richardson."

APPENDIX.

"Lille, France, January, 1870.

"Had the practical suggestion and application of nitrous oxide gas by Sir
"Humphry Davy been followed up by the surgical profession at the date of his
"researches (1800), no one would contend, or even pretend, that the merit
"of the anæsthetic discovery did not belong alone to that illustrious chemist.

"It is perfectly true that Sir Humphry Davy did not enter into the physio-
"logy of the anæsthetic condition induced; nor did he ever produce a coma-
"tose state. His experiments were confined to the first stage, that of *excitement*,
"and *he confined* his idea to nitrous oxide gas.

"When the negro 'Bob' had been rendered unconscious by the inhalation of
"the fumes from rum in December, 1839, and whose femur had been dislocated,
"which was reduced prior to his return to a state of consciousness, this was
"so remarkable a phenomenon as to elicit the special attention of my father and
"myself. All the cases of ordinary intoxication, where men had received
"severe injuries without any apparent sensibility, were discussed. It was
"at this time that the physiology of brain in this connexion first suggested
"thoughts which ultimately resulted in a fixed conviction, that *the inhalation
"of narcotic and stimulating vapours, by increasing the action of the lungs, caused
"a nervous congestion of brain* which deprived the surface of the ordinary supply
"of *sentient* nervous fluid. When I stated to my father the fact of my having
"been rendered *insensible* by the *inhalation* of *sulphuric ether* in the chemical
"lecture room of the University College, London, our conviction was estab-
"lished that nearly all the stimulating gases and vapours would when inhaled
"produce a state of unconscious insensibility.

"In the following year (1840), at Charlestown, South Carolina, I made some
"experiments in corroboration of these conclusions. In 1841 my time was
"occupied in the investigation of the phenomena called Animal Magnetism, which
"eventuated in the Report of the Boston Committee, composed of the principal
"members of the medical, clerical, and legal professions.

"I never claimed anything for animal magnetism, but met my audiences as
"an investigator in common with themselves. Committees were invariably
"appointed by the audience, and the experiments made at their suggestion through
"the medium of the committee appointed.

"In the autumn of 1841 every species of *surgical operation* was performed
"during the *anæsthetic* state, induced by the mesmeric process; these were
"published. It was not, however, until 1842 that the special subject of the
"inhalation of narcotic and stimulating vapours claimed my attention, in
"order to repeat the feats of the Egyptian magicians. Of course I did not
"omit repeating in the lectures the experiments on myself of inhaling sul-
"phuric ether at the London University College, and the case of the negro
"'Bob,' in Louisiana, in 1839. These anecdotes were always a feature in my
"lectures. On several occasions, both in Philadelphia and Boston, I passed power-
"ful electric charges through persons rendered unconscious by the *inhalation of
"narcotic and stimulating vapours*, to demonstrate the unconscious state pro-
"duced. On one occasion, in the month of April, 1843, Dr. Hare, Professor of
"Chemistry, University of Pennsylvania, assisted me in these experiments.

APPENDIX.

"It was at this time that I wrote the passage in my work 'Psychography,' "published in Philadelphia, May, 1843 :—

"'THE POWER TO PRODUCE THE CONGESTIVE OR UNCONSCIOUS STATE OF BRAIN "IS *not confined to* the nervo-vital fluid of a second person. THE SAME STATE OF "THINGS MAY BE BROUGHT ABOUT BY *mental* excitement, accompanied by "muscular action—THE INHALATION OF NARCOTIC AND STIMULATING VAPOURS.' "Not, however, content with proving the entire insensibility by the aid of "electricity, I publicly extracted teeth during this anæsthetic state induced by "*inhalation.*

"I at that time considered the state thus brought about to be *identical* with "that of *mesmeric coma,* and in proof of which fact I state at page 27 of "'Psychography' (1843) that the condition of the pythoness or priestess who "*inhaled the fumes* in the Delphic Temple to be IDENTICAL with that of the "mesmerized person. The same words are repeated by me in explaining the "condition of the persons who were rendered insensible by the inhalation of "narcotic fumes in the feats performed by the Egyptian magicians. The "circumstance of the surgical profession not having taken advantage of my "published statements and public experiments, that 'the inhalation of narcotic "and stimulating vapours produces an anæsthetic state, does not mitigate as "to the priority, or render my discovery of less value.

"It is most certain that had they done so in 1842 and 1843, no one would "have disputed my claim. Individually I took every means to promulgate "these facts to the world. I lectured and performed experiments on inhalation "in all the principal cities of the United States, Canada, Liverpool, and London. "Did any of those who followed me in 1844 and 1846 explain the physiology "of the nervous system, especially the condition of the brain, which I had pre- "viously done?

"I cannot imagine how Horace Wells, or those who vindicate his claim, can "attribute any merit in his having inhaled nitrous oxide, and had a tooth ex- "tracted, which he had seen administered by Mr. Coulton the previous "evening.

"It is admitted that Mr. Wells was not a man of education, nor had he any "scientific information as to the properties of protoxide of nitrogen. Had he "been acquainted with the physiology of the brain and nervous system, he "would have rendered the persons UNCONSCIOUS. We have the most positive "evidence that he did not administer the gas beyond the stage of *excitement*, as "Dr. P. W. Ellsworth, in writing to the *Boston Medical and Surgical Journal,* "distinctly states (June 18th, 1845) : 'THE PATIENTS APPEAR VERY MERRY "DURING THE OPERATION, and no unpleasant effects FOLLOW THE USE OF THE "NITROUS OXIDE GAS.' Nothing can be more plain than that UNCONSCIOUSNESS "was never induced; there was only a *partial* anæsthetic state. How is it that "Dr. Ellsworth makes no mention of the use of sulphuric ether by Mr. Wells? "This is most important, as showing how extravagantly Mr. Wells wrote in "*Galignani's Messenger* when in Paris in February, 1847, AFTER he had heard "of Morton's extraction of teeth during an anæsthetic state, induced by the "inhalation *of ether.* It was only then that for the first time he says:—'I "have administered the nitrous oxide and the *vapour of ether* to about fifty

K 2

APPENDIX.

"'persons.' Not a single document can be produced in confirmation of this "statement.

"It is a curious anomaly that Morton, who was a partner of Wells, should "not have ever heard of this administration of ether. For it is beyond all ques-"tion that Morton had got his idea from a Mr. Speires, who had seen ether "given at the Lexington University, in lieu of nitrous oxide gas, to the students; "the same as I had seen and experienced several years previously administered "by Dr. Turner, Professor of Chemistry at the London University.

"When Morton called on Dr. Jackson, he in all probability merely required *a* "*suitable apparatus*, in order to administer the *sulphuric ether*. This must be "the conclusion of all impartial critics. As to the story he invented about having "made experiments on a Newfoundland dog prior to this period, there does not "appear the least probability as to its being true.

"Had he made these prior experiments, he never would have been so anxious "and shown such ignorance relative to where he could *obtain the sulphuric* "*ether*, and 'what kind of stuff it was!' Dr. Jackson indicated to him that it "could be purchased at Burnett's, where he, Morton, accordingly went and pur-"chased the ether. This fact has been proved beyond all question. Now it "follows that Morton was entirely ignorant of its properties at this time— "that is, when he went to Dr. Jackson, or as to where the *proper ether* could be "obtained. This part of the history is equally prejudicial to the *vaunting* asser-"tion of Wells *in* 1847, that he had 'administered *the ether to fifty persons.*'

"The constant disposition to romance and indulge in exaggerations is too "manifest both on the part of Horace Wells and W. T. G. Morton. They "were both entirely ignorant of the physiology of the action of the anæsthetic "agents, even at the time of taking out the letters patent, for these words are "used,—'THERE IS VERY NEARLY, if not entire absence of all pain.'

"Dr. McIntyre says, 'That when Morton was leaving, Dr. Jackson said, "I "will tell you what will answer as well as nitrous oxide gas. Morton asked "what it was. Dr. Jackson told him to go to Burnett's and get some pure "sulphuric ether, pour it on a handkerchief and cause the patient to inhale it. "*Morton asked what sulphuric ether was*, what sort of *looking stuff it was!* I "stayed in the front room while Morton and Jackson went to look at the ether. "I am satisfied he knew nothing about its properties or nature. I heard "Morton ask Dr. Jackson very particularly whether it would be safe to "use. Dr. Jackson assured him that it was perfectly safe, and alluded to the "students at Cambridge having used it. Morton appeared to be afraid to use "the ether, and asked him several times if it was safe. Dr. Jackson advised "Morton to try it on himself. Morton asked me if I would be willing to try "it. I told him I would.'

"It is conclusive that if Morton had known anything of the chemical pro-"perties of sulphuric ether, he never would have gone to Dr. Jackson at all. "The very fact of his going proves two things, that he had never made any "previous trials, as he has since stated, and secondly, that sulphuric ether was "not known to Horace Wells, who was Morton's partner. Vide *Galignani's* "*Messenger*, February 15th, 1847.

"As I have said before, these experiments both of Horace Wells with "nitrous oxide, and Morton with sulphuric ether, were mere casual, hap- "hazard trials; there was no inductive reasoning, no scientific knowledge "exhibited, neither in the one case nor the other.

"My public experiments in 1842 and 1843 with alcohol, sulphuric ether, "stramonium, poppy head and seeds, coriander seeds, &c., the fumes of which "were inhaled, and a complete state of unconsciousness produced, had at least "the merit of having been arrived at from my knowledge of the physiology of "the brain and nervous system. The sudden, I may add magical adoption "by the medical profession in 1846 and 1847 of the necessity of producing a "state of anæsthesia, so that surgical operations could be performed painlessly, "cannot disturb the remarkable announcement by Sir Humphry Davy in 1800:—

"'As nitrous oxide in its extensive operation seems capable of destroying physi- "cal pain, it may probably be used with advantage during surgical operations in "which no great effusion of blood takes place.'

"Certainly these words admit of no ambiguity; they were published by one of "the most illustrious of England's most distinguished men of *science*, and yet "not a member of the profession takes the trouble to make experiments in con- "firmation. I cannot therefore be surprised after this inexplicable apathy "that my public experiments from 1841 to 1844 should have remained *unheeded*. "How is it that the experiments made by Horace Wells before Dr. Warren's "medical class, in the month of January, 1845, also had no effect in arousing "the medical profession?

"Had not Morton associated himself with Dr. Charles T. Jackson in "1846, and taken out *letters patent*, I doubt much if the profession to this "day would have recognised the necessity of inducing the anæsthetic state. "It was the mysterious charlatanry of the patent business of Morton and "Jackson which induced its adoption.

"It is positively certain that I induced an anæsthetic state for surgical "operations in 1841, 1842, 1843. Had I *not* done so then there might be "raised the question as to the right or justice of my name being associated "with the anæsthetic discovery. But as I took every available opportunity "to publish these facts for the benefit of my fellow-men without dreaming of a "patent, there is no reason why my name should not be connected with a "discovery which is an aid of incalculable importance to the science of "surgery, in rendering the patient perfectly passive during operation. It is a "discovery which has from the earliest ages been mythically and poetically "dreamt of. Its realization and adoption render it the greatest blessing "which man has in his power of applying to his suffering fellow-being, to "obviate the physical agony and mental dread incidental to surgical operations. "In 1839 Velpeau, one of the most distinguished French surgeons, said, 'To "avoid pain in surgical operations is a chimera, which cannot be permitted to "be entertained or sought for.'

"Yours truly,

"ROBERT H. COLLYER, M.D.

" To Sir J. Y. Simpson, Bt., Edinburgh."

APPENDIX.

The following advertisement appeared in the *Medical Times* and *Lancet*, of January, 1847, and other periodicals of the same date. For audacity and charlatanry, it eclipses any advertisement I ever read:—

"PATENT LETHONIC APPARATUS.

"Notice is hereby given, that making, using, or vending, in England, without licence from me, the Apparatus for the Inhalation of Ether, of which a description and a drawing were given in the *Medical Times* of January 9th instant, page 290, and in which a valve or valves prevent the return of vapour, once inhaled, into the vessel containing the ether, and sponge is used to increase the evaporating surface, is A DIRECT INFRINGEMENT of the Patent secured on the invention named the Letheon ; and ALL PERSONS ARE HEREBY CAUTIONED against making, using, or vending, without such licence, that or any similar apparatus."

"THE LETHEON.

To the Editor of the "Lancet."

"London, 18, Duke Street, St. James's, Jan. 6th, 1847.

"SIR,—I am informed that the name 'THE LETHEON' has been given by the Inventors in the United States, to the means of procuring insensibility to pain for surgical purposes. The apparatus is called 'The Letheonic Apparatus ;' the surgeon is said 'to Lethonize ;' the patient to be 'Lethonized.' The derivation, from the river Lethe, the waters of which, according to Greek mythology, caused oblivion in the memory of the person who drank, seems to be appropriate.

"In the *Lancet* of January 2nd, I gave notice of having accepted the agency of affairs concerning the Patent for England and the Colonies, and stated that I should adhere to such a course, that no charge of illiberality could rest upon the proprietors of the Patent or upon myself.

"Seeing the great importance, as well as feeling the delicacy of questions likely to arise, relating to the amount and form of compensation to be given by the public for the use of the invention, and their bearings upon common humanity, as well as upon private rights, I have undertaken the agency of the Patent in the belief and confidence that I could reconcile the just claims of the inventors and their representatives, with the expectations and wishes of an intelligent and liberal profession.

"In furtherance of these views, I now give public notice to the Governors or Trustees of all free or charitable Hospitals, Infirmaries, and Dispensaries in England and Wales, that I will grant licences to use the invention for any and all purposes within the walls of the respective Institutions, during the full term of the Patent, to each Hospital, Infirmary, or Dispensary, for Five Guineas.

"I except from these terms institutions belonging to Government, because it is to be expected that Government will, for a licence to use the invention for Government purposes, and particularly in the army and navy, voluntarily

APPENDIX. 135

"offer a compensation in some degree commensurate with the merit and value
"of the invention.

"It is not my intention to grant licences to any individuals, except to duly
"qualified surgeons and physicians, and to dentists solely for dental uses; and
"I desire that no surgeon or physician shall be excluded from the use of the
"invention, by reason of the amount of tax demanded.

"I therefore give further notice, that I will grant to any surgeon or physician,
"not being a professional dentist, a licence to use the invention in his private
"and personal practice, in the county in which he resides, for the sum of One
"Guinea per annum, or of Five Guineas for seven years, or of Eight Guineas
"for the whole term of the Patent, time to commence from January 1st, 1847.

"A charge of One Guinea only will be made to all Licencees, corporate or
"private, for the legal conveyance of rights; and for the protection of
"Licencees as well as of the Patent, all Licencees will be required to furnish
"themselves with apparatus from agents of sale to be specially appointed, so
"soon as such agents shall be ready to supply apparatus needed.

"I have adopted this scale of low charges for the purpose of bringing the
"question of liberality or illiberality to a prompt and decisive test. Should the
"advances herein made not be met in a similar spirit, a different policy will be
"pursued, and the advantages now tendered will be withdrawn.

"JAMES A. DORR,
"Agent for the Proprietors of the Patent."

Is it not monstrous that Drs. Morton and Jackson, the proprietors of the patent, through their agent Mr. Dorr, should have committed such an act; where is the philosophical, scientific spirit which should have instigated them, had they been original discoverers?

The "great discovery" is made a trading affair, and is commenced by being thus heralded to the world, and trafficking on the ills and aches of our common nature. The very fact of taking out a patent in the United States, Great Britain, France, and other countries, advertising in all the newspapers, shows most conclusively that Drs. Jackson and Morton were merely prompted by sordid mercenary motives. The idea of these "Discoverers" selling licences, one guinea per annum, or five guineas for seven years, and eight guineas for fourteen years, the whole term of the patent, from each medical man! This would have yielded a splendid income, even from London alone, which numbers several thousand medical practitioners.

The moment the news arrived in December, 1846, that a patent had been applied for, the author of this pamphlet, knowing himself to be the original discoverer, gave it *at once*, without hesitation to the public, never dreaming of making a speculation of anæsthesia.—*Vide* original letter page 16.

APPENDIX.

Copy of the Copyright of "Psychography."

(L S) Eastern District of Pennsylvania, to wit. Be it remembered that on the first day of June, Anno Domini one thousand eight hundred and forty three, Robert H. Collyer, M.D., of this district, has deposited in this office a book, the title of which is in the words following, to wit: *Psychography or the Embodiment of Thought.* The right whereof he claims as author in conformity with an Act of Congress entitled: An Act to amend the several Acts respecting Copyrights.

IRA HOPKINSON,
Clerk of the District.

1843, June 2nd, Copy of work deposited.

J. BENOHEND.

The Hon. Truman Smith says, "It is not at all improbable, that had Wells "lived and had the boldness to follow up his early *successful* experiments, "chloroform and ether would never have been thou lit of as an anæsthetic."

Then Mr. Smith admits that Wells did not follow up his early successful experiments, nor did he use ether. Had these early experiments of January, 1845, *been successful,* he would have followed them up. It was the want of success which caused him to abandon them.

It is also very evident that neither Dr. Charles T. Jackson nor his *conjoint patentee* knew anything of the physiology of anæsthesia, or they would not have used such language in their patent as, "There is very little or very nearly an entire absence of pain. . . . . With any or very little pain, or giving the patient any apparent or real pain, or so little in comparison to that produced in the usual process of conducting surgical operations, as to be scarcely noticeable."

I might have expected from such a man as Dr. Charles T. Jackson (who from *his own account* had produced *unconsciousness* years before in *strict privacy*), a *more philosophical explanation.* The truth is, neither Jackson nor Morton at this date had the least idea of producing a state of anæsthesia, as is now understood; for in their patent they also say, "We sometimes combine a narcotic pre- "paration, such as opium or morphine, with the ether. This may be done by "any ways known to chemists, by which a combination of etheric and narcotic "vapours may be produced." Immortal Jackson ! you really ought to have given the formulæ of these mysterious combinations.

Review of the "Lancet's" Article, of June 11th, 1870, "History of Anæsthetic Discovery."

When it is remembered that even in 1839 the medical profession considered the sufferance of pain as a necessary and even beneficial accompaniment to surgical operations, it is not surprising that my early investigations received no encouragement from the profession. One of the most eminent French surgeons,

Velpeau, says, in 1839 :—"*To do away with pain in surgical operations is a visionary impossibility, which is now not permitted to be thought of; the cutting instrument and pain in surgical operations are two things which cannot be presented to the mind of the patient one without the other, and we are obliged to admit the necessary association—i.e., pain and surgical operations.*"

When as early as 1840 I first announced to the medical profession of Charlestown, South Carolina, that I had reduced a dislocation of the hip-joint some two months previously near New Orleans, without the patient having experienced the least pain—the patient being in a state of unconsciousness, induced by the inhalation of alcohol vapour—no one gave the least credence to my statement of the fact, or believed it possible that a person could be rendered insensible by *inhalation*, so that one of the most difficult and painful operations could have been performed without consciousness of the patient.

Having, however, been convinced of the truth of the physiological fact that insensibility was induced by inhalation, the ridicule and incredulity with which my statements were everywhere received had no effect in altering the conviction of my senses, and so far from deterring me, the very opposition induced a fixed determination to investigate the whole subject of anæsthesia. I had already been convinced that a person could be rendered insensible during a comatose state, known as animal magnetism. This fact was not admitted by any one at that period. These circumstances awoke thoughts such as these. Is it possible that truths so easily demonstrated are denied by every one? Surely as they are truths, they must have some beneficial application.

After two years' systematic investigation, I had classified the mode of producing an anæsthetic state under five distinct heads —1st. The result of great natural fatigue. 2nd. By the transmission of the nervous fluid from one person to another. 3rd. The concentration of the mind on one subject accompanied by muscular action. 4th. By gazing steadily on an object. 5th. By the inhalation of narcotic and stimulating vapours. It was thought by me at the time that these conditions of brain were identical. My opinions have materially changed in this regard.

It must be remembered that I was treading entirely new ground; receiving no aid from any one. On the contrary, my efforts were received with every discouragement from a mocking and scoffing world.

Of course, now that nearly thirty years of *experience* has been bought, it is wonderfully easy to assume an oracular wisdom, and state what might or might not have been done. Any man can become a Solomon after events have occurred; nor does this *ex post facto* advice demand much judgment. It is intolerant pedantry for any man to pretend to say what he would have done had he been placed under circumstances so exceptional in their character. After a great principle has been propounded and established, every one seems astonished at the simplicity of the means employed in arriving at the discovery.

It is the old story of Columbus and the egg. "*Nothing* is more easy when you once know how to do it." After the discovery of the great Continent of

APPENDIX.

America, nothing was more easy than to discover individual parts. The difficulty was to fight the original battle, to establish the fact that the inhalation of narcotic and stimulating vapours produced *an anæsthetic state.*

This fact was published by me in May, 1843. Until a prior publication is produced, it would be just as reasonable to state that Galileo did not discover the satellites of Jupiter, or Sir Isaac Newton the laws of gravity, as that I am not the discoverer that the *inhalation of narcotic vapours produce an unconscious state.* As this matter admits of direct proof, controversy as to priority is out of the question; it is years in advance of every other claimant.

When the writer in the *Lancet* used these words: "*The lectures and works of Dr. Collyer were of a kind, we must candidly say, not calculated to arrest seriously the attention of the profession at the time,*" he evidently had forgotten that the suggestion of Sir Humphry Davy, forty years prior, had not *arrested* the attention of the profession. Even when Horace Wells, in January, 1845, made the experiment before Dr. Warren's medical class in Boston, the attention of the profession was not arrested.

It is difficult to conceive what would have arrested the attention of the profession.

I have only to refer to the fact, that when Dr. William Harvey announced to the medical profession that he had discovered the circulation of the blood—it is a notorious fact, stated by contemporaneous history—that hardly a medical man of the time gave his adherence to the discovery.

The history of Dr. Jenner is another example of the curious obstinacy with which new discoveries are received. Vaccination even now, in 1871, has a battle to fight against the perversity and obtuseness incidental to humanity.

It was *the wonderful secret* and the *conjoint patent business* of Morton and Jackson, combined with all kinds of the most audacious charlatanry, which caused the medical profession to adopt the principle of producing anæsthesia by inhalation of ether.

It was only on the 20th of December, 1846, that the European public became acquainted with Morton's experiments with ether, which dated from the 30th of September. In fine, ten weeks are allowed to elapse before divulging *the secret,* and securing letters patent.

That my lectures, as stated by the writer in the *Lancet,* did not arrest the attention of the profession is so singularly contrary to the fact, that I am forced to republish a few extracts.

Cheltenham Examiner and Looker-on, February, 1844.—"Dr. Collyer's "lecture at the Assembly Rooms on Thursday evening differed essentially from "that delivered at the Literary Institution, which was of a purely scientific and "professional character, for the most part discussing the subject in a philo-"sophical spirit, whereas that of Thursday was altogether of a popular kind, "not entering into the *rationale* of the question."

Liverpool Mail, October 13th, 1843.—"Thus ended the first lecture, the "audience (a great portion professional) expressing themselves as being fully "convinced that Dr. Collyer was master of his subject and capable of throwing

"' a flood of scientific information in regard to departments which have remained "hitherto unexplained."

Liverpool Standard, October 14th, 1843.—"From want of space we are pre-"vented from giving a detailed account of Dr. Collyer's philosophical lecture." On all and every occasion I met committees of medical men, who witnessed my experiments. On one occasion—the investigations continuing for weeks—a resolution was *unanimously* passed, "That the experiments of Dr. Collyer were *not* to be accounted for on any physiological principle known to them."

The writer in the *Lancet* has, however, made *one error* which cannot be excused—namely, that of deliberate misrepresentation in reference to the *congestive state of brain*. Not content with the mistake made, he actually adds a note to bring it specially forward to notice; and adds with apparent innocence, "*Recent research has led to the opinion that during sleep and insensibility* produced by artificial means, the brain is probably deprived of blood rather than congested."

Now my words in 1842 and 1843 are "nervous *congestive state*," in contradistinction to congestion produced by an increased flow of blood to a part.

I had actually anticipated in 1842 what "*recent research*" has only now discovered!

In fine, there is a hidden mystery about this error or singular mistake which time will perhaps unravel. The philosophy of the nervous fluid being in excess causing a "nervous congestive state of brain," was the special topic of the lectures delivered in 1842, 1843, and 1844.

In 1840 I delivered a series of lectures and experiments in Baltimore with the nitrous oxide gas.

The fact of having performed surgical operations during an anæsthetic state in 1841—prior to the publication in 1843—is the strongest confirmation that my mind was occupied with that idea—namely, the application of anæsthesia to surgical operations. If mesmerism could be generally applied, and most people were susceptible of its influence, no one can doubt but it would be universally adopted in preference to every other mode of producing anæsthesia. No one ever heard of a death having been produced by *the nervous fluid* of a second person.

It was absolutely necessary to discover how far the mesmeric agency was applicable before resorting extensively to the use of alcoholic vapours. In fine, had the writer in the *Lancet* nearly caused the death of his own brother by causing him to inhale the fumes of Indian hemp and alcoholic vapours, as occurred to myself, he too might have paused before denouncing an *original pioneer*, who was comparatively groping in the dark without any prior experience to guide him. Even after the long experience of *millions* of cases, do we not *now*, in 1871, find chloroform and bichloride of methylene producing instantaneous *death?* These facts should cause *critics* to be careful and prudent in thus summarily denouncing an original investigator; or if not exactly denouncing, "*damning with faint praise.*"

"Dr. Collyer simply represents a constantly repeated figure in the history of "human effort. He is Prince Rupert to the life, not to mention other men of "similar impulsive genius in other ages and on different fields of labour."

It is impossible to discover the purport of this comparison. Most people, no doubt, would feel their vanity much flattered at being compared to a prince of any sort. Who was Prince Rupert? It seems that he was third son of Frederick, King of Bohemia, born in 1619, and received a military education. He commanded the cavalry of Charles I. of England during the Civil War, and on various occasions manifested the most daring valour; but his impetuosity and imprudence more than counterbalanced the effects of his bravery. At length, having surrendered Bristol to General Fairfax, the king dismissed him from his service. Prince Rupert became a naval commander, and during the reign of Charles II. obtained several decisive victories over the Dutch. After this he retired from the public service, and devoted himself to scientific pursuits. He invented "Prince's metal," improved the composition and strength of gunpowder, discovered the mode of fusing blacklead, and discovered the art of engraving in mezzotinto; besides this, he became Governor of the Hudson's Bay Company.

So far as the inventive part of his character is concerned, there may be points of similarity; otherwise there is not the least resemblance. "Comparisons are odious" at the best of times. Still, if the writer in the *Lancet* had chosen a person like Roger Bacon, it might be accepted as a compliment; but, of all men in the world, to be compared to a prince was an ill-chosen comparison. To shine by another's light proves you have not much of your own. The writer in the *Lancet* seems to have got into a muddle when he says:—"*Our own opinion is, that Collyer, a man of impetuous perception, im-*"*pulsive action, open nature, and unrestrainable fluency of speech, did originally* "seize such analogies as exist between the so-called hypnotic condition from "mesmerism, and the rapid narcotism produced by narcotic vapours; that he "laid himself out publicly to announce these analogies; that he succeeded in "securing a violent opposition, which made his peculiar views familiar to those "who were living near to the scene of the controversy; that he cried *first* hail "on a beat which he did not follow up efficiently. We have further no doubt, "that had he given up the mesmeric idea and proceeded systematically with "his plan of making the body insensible by *inhaling* the vapour of alcohol, "HE WOULD HAVE HAD NO ONE TO DISPUTE WITH HIM IN PRIORITY."

Who is it then that disputes the priority?

It cannot be Wells or Morton, as their experiments were in December, 1844, and September, 1846, whereas the alcoholic inhalations were from 1839 to 1844. It is a fact which admits of no dispute, that in May, 1843, these words were published in Philadelphia, New York, and Boston, and re-copied in the Liverpool and London newspapers:—"That *the inhalation of narcotic and stimulating vapours* produced an insensible and unconscious state." Also, that from 1839 to 1844, all sorts of surgical operations were performed. At no time, regardless of trouble or expense, was an opportunity lost of demonstrating publicly the practicability of producing an anæsthetic state, so that surgical operations could be painlessly performed. The whole ground of anæsthesia was gone over years prior to every other claimant. It seems that the writer in the *Lancet* indulges in theories, speculations, and comparisons which have no

APPENDIX. 141

value because not in accordance with the facts as they occurred. He seems to have a playfully innocent manner of "putting one up, so as to more effectually knock one down." He actually seemed alarmed at his own temerity. When once the principle had been published that "the *inhalation* of narcotic and stimulating vapours" produced an unconscious state of brain, there was no great mental effort or merit in others putting the principle into practice, or varying the means of producing the like effect. Dr. Edward Jenner discovered that the lymph from the cow possessed anti-varioloid properties. Vaccination is found to counteract the susceptibility to small-pox. Here a great principle was demonstrated. It is not to be supposed that if any one were to innoculate from any other animal, a goat for instance, that any great merit would attend such a substitution of the lymph of the goat for that of the cow.

It is the want of liberality in confused expressions of this kind that is complained of:—

"We have further no doubt, that had he given up the mesmeric idea " and proceeded systematically with his plan of making THE BODY INSENSIBLE by inhaling the vapour of alcohol, *he would have had no one to dispute with him in priority.*"

As it is here admitted that the body was rendered *insensible by the inhalation of alcohol,* in 1842-1843, how the question of *priority* could be interfered with it is difficult to imagine.

Had the writer understood the true facts as they occurred, he never would have written in such a patronizing style. As no *anterior* publication has ever been produced to May, 1843, that "*the inhalation* of narcotic and stimulating vapours produce the nervous congestive state of brain," or anæsthetic state, I ask no sympathizing smiles, no merciful considerations, but a rigid examination of the facts as they existed prior to the date of every other claimant. No man has a right to pass judgment *carelessly* on his fellow-man because he happens to be entrusted with the editorship of an article on a special topic. The abuse of so sacred a trust is, to say the least, the rankest egotism.

Had the *Lancet* writer known the ordeal of persecution, ribald invective, and contumacious opposition to which I was subjected from the year 1840 to 1844, in the advocacy of the necessity of producing an anæsthetic state, so that surgical operations could be painlessly performed, he never would have written in such a *légère* and jaunty manner on a subject of such importance as the alleviation of human suffering.

The inveterate joker is, perhaps, the most dangerous of men; *coûte que coûte*, he must be funny in season and out of season. He is continually watching the opportunity to indulge in his sense of the humorous. There is a time for all things; to whistle an Irish jig at a funeral, or to offer up a prayer between the acts of a comedy, would be such violent antagonisms as to be *offensive.*

There was a judge, it is said, who would rather hang the prisoner than his leg of mutton should get cold; so it is with the writer in the *Lancet.* He would sooner sacrifice any one than not perpetrate his joke. At one moment Dr. Collyer is compared to Prince Rupert, at the next he is made to wander through the States with his negro "Bob;" the antithesis is perfect. It is the fable of the boys and the frogs. The old frog said to the boys, who were throwing stones, "It may be fun unto you, but 'tis death unto us."

It is the motto, "No matter who sinks, so long as we swim." Repulsive is that wrapt up egotism which measures everything from the standard of *self*.

Nothing is more facile than to reason *after events*, then every man is wise—as to what should or should not have been done. To reason from the experience of 1871 as to the course which ought to have been pursued in 1840 to 1844, is as consistent and reasonable as to expect an eminent physiologist like Dr. B. W. Richardson to perform his experiments from the standard of experience that will be obtained in 1900, or thirty years hence. Of course, those who are in existence in 1900 will be shocked at such announcements as these in the *Lancet* and other Journals of April 22nd, 1871 :—

"DEATH FROM CHLOROFORM.—At the Swansea Hospital, a few days ago, a "clog-maker named Barrett died under the influence of chloroform. Three "weeks ago he fractured his leg, and amputation being considered necessary, "the preparations were made with his consent. Before the operation com-"menced, and while inhaling the chloroform, he died."

"DEATH FROM CHLOROFORM.—Lieutenant Colonel Rogers, R. A., was stay-"ing with his brother at Cornwood, last week, and while in the garden at the "back of the house, fell over a plant-pot, thereby receiving a compound frac-"ture of the leg and a dislocated ankle. The broken bones were set by two "medical gentlemen of Plympton, but Colonel Rogers not progressing, a third "doctor was called, and it was determined that the leg should be reset while "the Colonel was under the influence of chloroform. The latter was adminis-"tered and caused almost instant death."—*Times, May* 15*th*, 1871.

"DEATH FROM BICHLORIDE OF METHYLENE.—Mr. Bedford held an inquest "yesterday at the Charing-cross Hospital on the body of David Skelton, a "labourer, aged 41, who died while under the influence of methylene, after "undergoing an operation. Mr. Edwin Canton, surgeon to Charing-cross "Hospital, stated that he attended the deceased on his admission to the hospi-"tal, and found the bones of one of the fingers on the left hand extensively "diseased from an injury he had received from a pig's tusk. With the exception "of the bad finger the deceased was in excellent bodily health, and was a "strong muscular man. He advised the deceased to have his finger removed, "to which he consented, and said he should wish to be under the influence of "chloroform while the operation was being performed. On Tuesday last the "operation took place, the deceased having previously inhaled $1\frac{1}{2}$ drachms of "methylene, which was more generally used as a substitute for common chloro-"form. The methylene was administered in the presence of witness by the regular "administrator of the hospital, a gentleman of large experience. The "quantity administered was not more than half that usually given. The "deceased having become insensible after inhaling the above quantity of "methylene, he (witness) removed the finger from his hand, the operation not "lasting more than one minute. It was then proved that the deceased's head "had fallen upon one side, his eyes were upturned, and breathing and pulsa-

"tion had ceased. Every means was at once adopted to restore animation, "but without effect. He had since made a *post mortem* examination and found "the brain and every other organ in a perfect state of health. There was "nothing whatever to account for death. There was not the slightest trace of "any action of the methylene on either the heart or brain, the organs mainly "affected by chloroform when administered. The only way he could account "for the man's death was, that being in a state of great nervous excitement at "having to undergo the operation, the methylene had acted upon the nervous "system, producing instant death. He had known death to have resulted "under an operation from the nervous excitement of the patient, without chloro-"form having been inhaled. There was no doubt that the death of the "deceased had been produced by the methylene he had inhaled. The cases of "death while under the influence of methylene were extremely rare. In all "probability the deceased would have survived the operation had it been per-"formed without his inhaling the methylene, which was administered at his "own request. He never allowed methylene to be administered to a patient "about to undergo an operation unless with the patient's full consent after due "deliberation. The Jury returned the following verdict :—' That the deceased "died from the effects of methylene properly administered during an opera-"tion."—*Standard, April 22nd,* 1871.

Hundreds of similar cases could be adduced. This is the answer why, in 1840 to 1844, thirty years since, the anæsthetic investigation was not *systematically* proceeded with according to the ideas and experience of 1871. If these awfully sudden deaths did not occur we might forgive this forgetfulness or rather uncharitableness on the part of writers, who lose sight of past difficulties in the advocacy of a new discovery. This severe criticism, however, recoils on itself. Had one of the above cases of instantaneous death in the experiments of *rendering the body insensible by alcoholic vapour* in 1840 to 1844 occurred, would the writer of the article in the *Lancet* have the temerity to state that the experimenter would *not* have been tried for murder, found guilty, and executed? Let him imagine, certainly not asking too much, the discovery in 1900, or thirty years hence, of an anæsthetic which will not be liable to produce such baneful results as chloroform and bichloride of methylene. It would not be noble or generous and manifest much magnanimity on the part of a writer in a medical journal who then, in 1900, would denounce Dr. B. W. Richardson or Sir James Simpson because of these untoward results in 1871.

It is so easy to find fault or see defects in others.

" Oh, wad some power the giftie gie us,
To see oursels as others see us,
It wad frae mony a blunder free us,
And foolish notion."

It should not be forgotten that, though no one could claim priority in experiments performed in 1840, 1841, 1842, and 1843, with no experience to guide, still not a single fatal result ensued, though frequently the most alarming condition was induced.

APPENDIX.

Note.—Between bichloride of methylene and chloroform there is a distinction without much difference; practically it is chloroform diluted. But the advocates of methylene claim for it, that it is more gentle in its action, that there is less *struggling*, less vascular excitement, its narcotic effects are equally prolonged, in fine, that it is as effective as chloroform, without any of its disagreeables.

If these are facts, the reason of the superiority of the methylene must result because of its containing *less chlorine* than the chloroform. Does not this fact lead to the conclusion that all compounds containing chlorine are liable to paralyse the heart's action, more especially in those whose nervous system indicates great sensibility. The inhalation of *ether* is not liable to the same dangers as either chloroform or methylene, its composition being carbon 4 atoms, hydrogen 5, oxygen 1. The only foreign agent to the respiratory organs being the hydrogen.

The most unobjectionable anæsthetic is without doubt the nitrous oxide, or protoxide of nitrogen gas. It is indeed a frivolous excuse, that because of the greater portability or convenient facility of administration of chloroform, methylene, or ether, that they should be used in preference to the nitrous oxide which, from its close analogy to atmospheric air, must at once recommend its use as an anæsthetic. The nearer we approach to the natural respiratory medium, in the same ratio do we reduce the mischances which jeopardize life itself, from the inhalation of an agent so foreign to the system as chloroform or methylene.

It is not to be supposed that I would entirely deprecate their use, but the administration must be so managed as to prevent such pungent vapours from acting *too suddenly*, and thus paralysing the great nervous centres in constitutions of special idiosyncrasy or nervous peculiarity. When the first shock to the nervous system has been overcome, NO SUBSEQUENT DANGER NEED BE APPREHENDED.

I am at this moment engaged in the construction of an inhaling apparatus, which I have every reason to believe will meet all the conditions required, so that the nervous congestive, or insensible state may be prolonged by the inhalation of the nitrous oxide gas to ten minutes, which is of sufficient duration for the great majority of surgical operations to be performed *painlessly*, without endangering, in any case, the life of the patient.

Time will demonstrate that the only anæsthetics which can with safety be administered, are those which increase the *vital condition* by producing a *true nervous congestion* of the brain and nervous centres. All those which *negative* or *depress*, must necessarily endanger life.

ROBERT H. COLLYER, M.D.

199, BROMPTON ROAD, S.W.
    Near South Kensington Museum.
      June, 1871.

THE END.

www.ingramcontent.com/pod-product-compliance
Lightning Source LLC
Chambersburg PA
CBHW022124160426
43197CB00009B/1148